SO WHAT'S THE POINT

A Primer for
True Spiritual Awakening

Bob Lively

TREATY OAK PUBLISHERS

PUBLISHER'S NOTE

This is a work of personal memoir and inspiration. All of the characters, business establishments, and events are based on the author's personal experiences. Individuals' names may have been changed to protect their privacy.

Printed and published in the United States of America

TREATY OAK PUBLISHERS

ISBN-10: 1-943658-23-4
ISBN-13: 978-1-943658-23-7

ACKNOWLEDGMENTS

This book would not have been possible without the technical assistance of my wife, Mary Lynn, and without the expertise of my gifted editor, Ms. Cynthia J. Stone. The beautiful cover that adorns this book comes from the artistic genius of my youngest brother, James K. Lively, while the cover design is the excellent work of graphic artist Kim Greyer.

Of course, no book can reach the public without a publisher, and this book was published by one of the best, Austin's own TREATY OAK PUBLISHERS, arguably Texas' best independent press.

ALSO BY BOB LIVELY

NON-FICTION

BY STREAMS OF WATERS
(a history of Presbyterian Mo-Ranch Assembly)

ON EARTH AS IT IS
(an early collection of *Austin American-Statesman* columns)

ON EARTH AS IT IS - Vol. II
(a later collection of *Austin American-Statesman* columns)

SIMPLE STEPS... COSTLY CHOICES

FIVE WAYS TO GET OFF THE PALE HORSE
A Handbook for Making Life Work

GOD HELP ME THROUGH TODAY
Psalm 23 Revisited

WAITING FOR BLUEBONNETS

A WALK WITH GOD THROUGH FORGIVENESS

A PORTRAIT OF A PRAYER

FICTION

THE THIN PLACE

In loving memory of:

Henry McKee Lively
Mary Alice Keeton Lively
and
John Edward Lively

SO WHAT'S THE POINT

A Primer for
True Spiritual Awakening

Preface

If you have picked up this book and turned enough pages to read this brief preface, you may have asked yourself, "Why did this guy choose an artist's rendering of Colorado's iconic Long's Peak to adorn the cover of a book titled **So What's The Point?**"

That's a good question, and if it did come to mind, it means you are not only curious, but also likely in sync with the spiritual journey that is reflected in my writing of this book.

Did I choose Long's Peak for the cover because I thought this mountain's majesty and beauty—painted so brilliantly by my gifted younger brother, Jim—would attract readers to the book's content? The answer is "Yes." I did consider this a clever marketing strategy in that his rendering of Our Lady of Guadalupe on the cover of my novel, **The Thin Place**, did indeed prove to be an attention grabber.

Or did I choose Long's Peak for the cover because I love this mountain? The answer here is also an unqualified and passionate, "Yes!" Because I do, indeed, love this mountain, and I have a life-long relationship with Long's Peak which began with getting uncomfortably close to being killed upon her rugged North Face in the 14th summer of my life.

That memorable July in 1961, my father invited me to climb with him to the high and distant summit of Long's Peak.

Although I was familiar with the ancient tale of a man named Abraham taking his son Isaac to another mountaintop in the cause of proving his own obedience to God, I never assigned so much as a moment's worth of worry to the idea that climbing Long's Peak might be a bit risky. After all, I was strong, agile, and within two months of my 15th birthday, so what was there to be concerned about?

And in those days, if my father asked anything of me, my response was automatic and positive. Like most teenage sons, I wanted my father's approval, and there was no way I would disappoint him by declining to venture with him to the very top of one of Colorado's most challenging "fourteeners."

After donning my well-worn basketball shoes and a pair of faded jeans, I pulled on a light sweater over my t-shirt. My heart was filled with a newfound determination.

My dad and I drove into the morning's moonless incipience until we arrived at the empty Long's Peak trailhead parking lot where we began our climb at about two a.m. By the time the sun rose to light the sheer east face of this magnificent peak, we had reached the base of the steep North Face at a place called The Boulder Field.

The Boulder Field is aptly named because, both in breadth and length of about a mile, it is one huge piece of granite piled upon another by the unrelenting forces of an ancient ice. While this square mile of rugged terrain is not particularly forbidding, traversing it requires hopping from one boulder to the next, and this is a feat that demands agility, one good decision after another, and a sturdy pulmonary system.

Dad and I were about halfway done with our boulder hopping when the western sky warned us of impending danger. My father, as the leader of this expedition, failed to heed the warning simply because climbing this big mountain was what he'd always dreamed of doing. We were less than a still-arduous mile from the summit, and there was no way my dad would allow a little rain to turn us back.

In his mind, nothing would stop us now. Absolutely nothing.

My father had remarkably few flaws, but the one that did at times afflict his judgment was an irrational and persistent optimism assuring him all was well, even when all was not even close to being well. But then, this man had endured the Great Depression with his family in a series of East Texas sharecropper shacks before deciding to be the first in our family even to attempt college. After graduating as his high school's salutatorian, he enrolled in Sam Houston State Teachers' College with absolutely no money, and for the next three years and three summers he worked various jobs to put himself through school.

After graduation, he accepted a high school teaching position in a small East Texas logging community, where after a mere nine months he was, at the age of twenty-two, promoted to the position of principal. By his wits and by what he always called his uncanny "good luck," he managed to flourish during The Second World War, and he returned to Texas as a commissioned officer to launch what over the next half century would become a legendary business career.

This man was more than a survivor; he was a veritable conqueror. And this mere mountain of some 14,000 feet represented nothing to one who believed he could accomplish anything, once he set his mind to it. And on this particular summer morning, his mind was set as firmly as those granite boulders.

At fourteen, I'd accomplished very little except to survive

junior high school, which in retrospect was actually no small accomplishment. But that is, perhaps, another story for another time.

A not-so-distant thunder rattled the big mountain enough to threaten to shake me off the big boulder upon which I stood. Furious flashes of lightning punished the mountain's western shoulder, and was followed by a wind so fierce I feared we'd both be blown all the way to Denver without once touching down anywhere between the huge rock upon which I stood and Colorado's capital city some fifty miles away.

At first I was so numbed by the icy gales, I failed to realize how thoroughly a horizontal rain soaked me as it pummeled The Boulder Field with a ferocity I thought nature reserved only for tornadoes and hurricanes. Above the cacophony of the storm's raging, I heard the impossible: My intrepid father was yelling for me to take cover. We were finished climbing, and now the issue was quite simply staying alive.

I was more than willing to take shelter as lightning swirled above our heads like searchlights scanning the heavens. We were at least three thousand feet above the tree line, with little to protect us from the storm now determined to kill us both. I dropped to my knees on the surface of a boulder the size of a Dallas mansion to make myself as small a target as possible. I cried more than I prayed, and after what seemed like an hour or more, my father's drenched and worried presence hovered above me like the only benign cloud in that furious sky.

Even though the smile he wore was both predictable and feigned, he failed to conceal the terror etched in his face. Once I recognized anxiety in the countenance of a man who had taught himself never to be governed by fear, I acknowledged the obvious.

We were about to die.

As calmly as if he summoned me to awaken for another day at school, he said through his forced smile, "Bobby, we need somehow to squeeze between these boulders and get as far down as possible."

In an instant, I pushed my numb feet into a narrow crevice separating a smaller boulder from the one upon which I had previously stood. I watched from my icy burrow as my father did the same. Soon he disappeared into another crevice not ten yards away.

With all the strength I could muster in my skinny adolescent body, I squirmed and squeezed into that crevice until I was at least half concealed from the fury I was certain would within minutes kill me. As I lay buried in several inches of sleet and now shivering uncontrollably, my father yelled one last word of instruction. "Get rid of any metal you have on you. And throw it away as far as possible."

In seconds, I undid my belt and hurled it as far as I could, which was no more than a mere five yards or so. Still braced on the elbow of my non-throwing arm, I managed to yell, "Dad, are we going to make it?"

His answer arrived before yet another crash of thunder rattled the mountain. "I don't know, son. I don't know."

It was to be the one time in my life when my ever-positive father would express doubt about his or his family's personal well being. Hearing his uncertainty, I collapsed once again into the shallow crevice where I prayed like never before.

In the next cold and horrifying hour, thunder rocked the mountain and lightning hit the Boulder Field with enough force to shatter granite boulders and send shards of rock flying in every direction. Had I not been so terrified, I would have found the sight fascinating to the point of amazing.

As I once more hunkered down into the crevice I was now convinced would be my grave, I did my best to construct a prayer, but I had to preface any authentic attempt with the confession that I really didn't know what it meant to pray beyond the rote and pithy recitations of piety I'd learned in childhood. I knew only that there was nothing left to do but to ask God to deliver us from the danger that threatened to kill us both. I knew nothing of theology, but I did remember from Sunday school that Jesus had once calmed a storm.

I decided that if he could do it two thousand years before, he could also do it in the summer of 1961. To no surprise, my primitive prayer was little more than begging God to have his Son calm this particular storm long enough for my father and me to descend the mountain. The more I begged, the more the storm raged, and the more lightning flung granite shards all over the Boulder Field, some hitting only feet from where I shivered beneath several inches of sleet.

Somehow I recalled our pastor had taught me to speak to God as I would to an adult who loved me and who wanted only what was best for me. "Make prayer a conversation," he had said. "And take time to listen to the mystery of it all."

Now convinced I would more likely die of hypothermia than by a lightning strike, I opened my conversation with a promise. I bargained with God as most human beings do when faced with the prospect of imminent death. "God, I will give my life to your will if you will save me from this storm."

At dusk, the storm decided to drift in an easterly direction and thereby bless with the gift of rain fields of standing wheat as well as acre upon acre of Colorado sugar beets. My father and I climbed out of the burrows we'd dug for ourselves and descended the mountain.

How seriously I took the promise I made back then in a moment of abject terror I will likely never know. I was young, immature, and terrified when I made this sacred vow to a God I'd been taught was unadulterated love, mercy, and grace.

In retrospect, my adolescence was in no way dissimilar from the norm. I entered high school as a kid who had made a sacred vow I suspected would somehow shape, if not determine, my destiny. Throughout high school, I made good grades and earned a reputation for being a shy, but solid kid, who could be trusted to do what was right. I kept my vow a closely guarded secret, lest my friends and family consider me a religious nut.

Two years after my graduation from high school, my older brother Bill and I returned to Long's Peak and reached the summit on a beautiful August day with no real problems. If the big mountain still had any secrets to reveal, she kept them to herself that day.

Sometime during the spring of my senior year in college, I came to the conclusion that our country's war in Vietnam was illegal, immoral, and inarguably opposed to God. Consequently, I chose to avoid it and to do whatever I could as a citizen to oppose it within the bounds of God's will. Following my graduation from college, the war in Southeast Asia still raged.

Giving no small amount of thought and worry to the matter, I realized our government had actually waged two separate wars simultaneously. One was against the communists in Vietnam, and the other against poverty here in the United States. I decided to enlist in the War on Poverty and oppose the Vietnam War, even if it meant a prison term. I considered applying to a seminary, but right away gave up the idea, because I in no way felt called to go into the ministry.

I mailed an application to Washington, beseeching the bureaucrats in Lyndon Johnson's "War on Poverty" to accept me into a newly cobbled together program known as the National Teacher Corps, and thereby, grant me a draft deferment for the duration of my service. For weeks and then months, stress mounted as I waited to receive a positive response to my application. Nothing came.

On June 1st of that summer, I instead received a letter from Washington informing me that my status with the Selective Service Board had been changed from my student deferment to I-A. On June 20th, I bid my family and my beautiful fiancée farewell and drove straight through from Dallas to the village of Glen Haven, Colorado, where I had been employed to work on a boy's ranch high in the Rockies.

Before my departure from Dallas, I instructed my mother to call me on the ranch's only phone if yet another letter arrived from Washington, either notifying me that I was to report for my induction into the United States Army or that I had been deferred to fight poverty through the art of public school teaching, something I had been both trained and certified to do.

Every evening after a day's work, I entered the ranch's office on my way to the dining hall and sat in a chair and stared at a phone that refused to ring unless heat lightning flashed in Wyoming, not a hundred miles away. If wishes could have caused a phone to ring, that phone would have rung itself into an early obsolescence.

But, of course, it did not ring. Night after night, the phone did not ring. It only sat on the director's desk in stony silence determined to make me insane with anxiety.

As I viewed it, this phone held my future in its cold, black plastic case. Either I would return to Texas, and get married and, in time, become a teacher in a poverty school system under the aegis of the National Teacher Corps, or I would invite my future wife to flee with me to Canada, where I hoped I might land a teaching job and live out the rest of my life as a refugee and as a fugitive.

Night after night, the phone remained silent as I imagined it now mocked me from its place on the desk. By August, I decided if the phone didn't ring very soon, I would call my fiancée and ask her to join me in Denver. Then I planned to notify my parents that we were taking off for Canada to seek sanctuary from a war predicated upon a monstrous lie.

I realized full well that if I fled, this country's government would seek to introduce me to its own harsh definition of justice, which in no way would resemble what the prophet Micah had in mind when he proclaimed, that what God requires of every human being is "to do justice, and to love kindness, and to walk humbly with your God." (Micah 6:8)

On a night I had decided not to stare at the phone, at last this silent tormentor rang during dinner. I froze as the director's wife, a sweet woman with the countenance of a saint, answered the call and returned to the dining room wearing a smile that assured me that the call was mine.

I rose from the table on legs that felt as though they would refuse to support my weight. Somehow I managed to reach the director's office. Taking the phone in one trembling hand, I muttered, "Hello."

From the other end came my mother's warm, familiar, and on this night, surprisingly cheery voice. With joy in her reassuring tone, she read to me the wonderful news that I had been accepted into The National Teacher Corps, and that I was to report in early September to Prairie View A& M University, a predominantly black school near Houston. There I would enroll in a special master's program in poverty education. Simultaneous to this training, I was to teach in an elementary school where economically deprived children comprised the majority of the student body.

I wept as I bid my mother good night. I returned to the dining room and did what I could to finish my dinner. With my appetite disappeared, I rose once more from the table and approached the director with an impossible request, permission to take a horse out of the barn for the night.

"What do you want a horse for?" he said in a gruff tone.

"I won't be able to sleep, so I'd like to be on Miller's Fork at first light tomorrow morning, catching a mess of rainbow trout."

To my astonishment, but only after his wife nudged him in the ribs, he agreed, and then said with a smile, "Just don't run off with one of my horses. I'd hate to call the sheriff and report you as a horse thief."

I nodded, then made my way to the tiny cabin I called home that summer where my fly rod waited in the rafters high above my bunk. Toting the rod and my creel, I walked to the barn to grab a big shovel I used a couple of days every week to clean out the place.

With a rare sense of joyful purpose, I hoisted the shovel to one shoulder and marched like the soldier I refused to be to a special place by the roaring river home to at least a billion night crawlers. Following one or two shovelfuls of dirt mixed with squirms, I placed more worms than I would need into a cardboard carton and headed to the corral to awaken my horse.

The horse, a sweet little mare named Goldie, and I negoti-ated our way in the dark to the top of Boark Ridge, about a half a mile from Miller's Fork. A sudden descent into the pitch-black valley below seemed far less appealing than it had back in the dining hall. I slid out of the saddle and removed the bit and bridle from the horse's head. For a while I held her by a make-shift halter rope, but remembering this special night was about freedom, I released even the rope.

With my back braced against a tall lodge pole pine, I listened for any sounds the night might wish to share with an interloper like me. I longed to hear a bull elk bugle, but the rut was still more than a month off. The night chose to remain, for the most part, silent, save for the whisper of an easy wind in the pine boughs above. Between the pine tree's whispers I listened to my grazing horse pulling lush sprigs of grass up from the roots.

This high country night would for the remainder of my life be for me the very definition of perfect serenity and the pinnacle of what it could possibly mean to experience that biblical peace that surpasses all understanding. Filled with a joy I didn't know was possible, I decided this new day would be forever marked in my mind by the word liberation.

I was now free from the burden of participating, and quite possibly dying, in a war so wrong that many people described it as a horrendous national sin second only to the genocide of the Native Americans in the severity of its evil consequences. Consequently, I even freed the night crawlers so they might dig new burrows on the ridge top before the predator Colorado jays, magpies, and robins could swoop down upon them as the day worn on.

No, this was not to be a day for killing, so I even gave up the idea of catching the fat rainbow and cutthroat trout waiting for me in deep pools behind the myriad beaver dams on Miller's

Fork.

As I basked in the contentment that attends joy, the first streaks of the new morning filled the new day with more promise than I ever thought possible. Suddenly life was good again. I could now return safely to Texas and get married later that fall and enjoy a good life. Still braced against the rough bark of the lodge pole pine, I shifted to watch Goldie savor her freedom in the midst of the tall buffalo grass.

And that's when I saw it.

The sun lit Long's Peak like she was a distant torch on fire with the truth that "God is love." (1st John 4:8) Although she was miles away, I could make out every feature of her craggy face. Immediately below her flat magnificent summit lay a snow patch in the shape of a dove, a biblical symbol of the Holy Spirit.

The sight took my breath even more than the climb I'd made to her boulder field seven years before. I stood in abject reverence. "That's the most beautiful sight I have ever seen, or will ever see." (I later revised that observation the morning I first glimpsed the seven pounds of beauty that was my newborn daughter, Sarah.)

As I pondered the magnificence of Long's Peak in the new morning of August of 1968, I imagined I could hear the sounds of war and the suffering that is its evil handiwork. Before I could launch into another prayer of gratitude, I recalled my Boulder Field vow, and eighteen months after that unforgettable morning of freedom and following one year in The National Teacher Corps, I enrolled as a full-time student in Austin Presbyterian Theological Seminary.

After 40 years, I retired as a Presbyterian minister, and today I do my best to visit Long's Peak at least once a year so I might remember my vow to devote my life to God's will.

I can't say with even a hint of any integrity that I've come close to keeping the vow I made so long ago on Long's Peak, but I can say this: for the whole of my life, I've been blessed far, far beyond what I've ever deserved.

---RDL

CHAPTER 1

The Question

More than a decade ago, a boyhood friend contacted me to grieve with our family the loss of my younger brother and also catch me up on his life since the last time I'd seen him, about twenty-five years ago. As he released my hand following a vigorous handshake at my beloved brother's graveside, the uncharacteristic somberness of his tone and the intense anguish encompassed his eyes like an old wood frame left too long in the Texas sun.

He first told me he and his wife had divorced, a sad fact for which he surprised me by claiming total responsibility. In both my pastoral and personal experience, few men do that.

He next stunned me with what sounded like a clumsy, and excruciatingly painful, confession of his attempt at suicide. Of all the countless people who comprised the fabric of my happy childhood experience growing up on the so-called " wrong side" of the Trinity River in Dallas, Texas, in a blue collar section of the city known as Oak Cliff, he was one of the very last I thought might have ever considered suicide.

When we shared that turbulent era known as adolescence, I regarded him as one of the most talented and capable guys on the short list of my very good friends. He was an excellent student, who was generally regarded as a "real catch" by the young ladies who shared the halls and classrooms of our high school. He was a talented athlete who could knock loose the fillings of any receiver foolish to attempt to catch an old, beat-up, over-inflated football on any Oak Cliff sandlot. He was talented enough to play the coveted position of free safety.

But what made him even more special was his amazing voice. This young man possessed musical gifts equal to those who dominated the folk music scene of the early sixties. In fact, his ability with an acoustic guitar was legendary long before he graduated with honors from our venerated old blue-collar high school.

He once even rode with me all the way to Northern Colorado where I had helped him land a job as a summer camp counselor at the same high-end enterprise that had employed me the two previous summers. Our sojourn together out of the hot flatlands of Texas and into the high country of the Colorado Rockies turned out to be a pleasant adventure where we mixed memories with aspirations in the front seat of my tiny Corvair, a car consumer advocate Ralph Nader would later famously declare as "unsafe at any speed."

I saw it this way: If any two boys can remain friends after traveling together close to one thousand miles in the unforgiving front seat of a 1965 Chevrolet Corvair, their bond is likely indestructible.

And what changed a miserable—not to mention interminable—journey into joy was this young man's delightful spirit fueling a conversation riddled with interesting and carefully crafted insights into the great mystery that is life. He was a delightful traveling companion, who sometimes even broke into a spontaneous song whenever moved by the muse in his soul.

Moments before he approached me, I had attempted in vain to officiate at my younger brother's graveside service without sobbing. This long-time friend posed the single most penetrating question I have heard in more than forty years in the ministry.

After assuring me that he was now safe with himself, he said, "So what's the point?"

If I attempted some kind of feeble, reflexive response, I don't recall what it was. I did give him a hug and wish him well. Then I turned to greet the other mourners who had come to that mercilessly hot Dallas cemetery to comfort our family in what was thus far the darkest day of our life together.

What did his question really ask? And why did it so penetrate my soul and haunt me for the next decade?

The most honest answer is, "I really don't know."

That said, I have a hunch I have attributed far more power to his simple, if still a bit obtuse, question than he intended or that it deserved. Nevertheless, on my long, sad two-hundred-mile drive from Dallas to Austin, my friend's question flapped about in my soul like a desperate hawk snared by cruelty.

"So what is the point?" I asked myself over and over again once I was home and preparing to go before our local denominational body (Mission Presbytery) to request an honorable retirement designation. That way, I would receive a small check each month from the Presbyterian Board of Pensions.

Beyond being more than a little neurotic in accepting far too much responsibility for negative events in my life, I had also allowed his question to serve as an evaluative, and even indicting, metric of my life for the past 40 years. During those years I had frequently asked myself, "So what was the point of all the heart and soul I poured into the work I did for more than four decades?"

In moments of rigorous honesty I had to admit that my decision to go into the ministry had cost my family and me enormously. My wife, who is a retired university associate dean, once enjoyed singing in the church choir and serving on church committees and boards, but no longer attends worship or expresses any interest whatsoever in belonging to a church. My adult daughter would probably rather have a root canal than join another church, and my precious pre-school grandson, Henry, has never been baptized, and may never be.

In my more lucid moments, I realize my family's decision to turn away from the church is a defensive move predicated upon the healthy desire not to be hurt yet one more time. However, the moments that torment me all too frequently are when I convince myself their decisions are a result of my personal shortcomings and numerous failures as a minister.

The only Presbyterian Church I ever served was an old downtown congregation. In ten years of often seven-days-a-week service, I joined with others to found a soup kitchen for the homeless, an all-night shelter for the same population, a free housing program for so-called "street families," a battered women's shelter, a free psychotherapy program for women incarcerated in the Dallas County Jail, a Saturday Christian education program for minority children from the poorest neighborhoods, and a summer day camp for the same children. For this work, I received no small amount praise from the world, including recognition by the Dallas City Council and even the Governor of Texas.

Such praise filled a void in my soul driven by several unconscious longings I've never fully understood, but can no longer deny. In fact, a psychiatrist once suggested I was so passionate about feeding the hungry because I myself was hungry—not for food, but rather for recognition. In retrospect, I've come to believe he was exactly right.

For the most part, I discovered meaning in the work I was privileged to do in that old church in downtown Dallas, but I had to ask myself: was feeding and sheltering those whom Jesus called "the least of these" the point of my existence or my own unique *raison d'être*? Was this the reason I was born?

I used my own life experience as my guide and rejected the idea that at conception each of us is somehow mysteriously assigned a unique purpose (and subsequent mission) for our lives. No, I told myself, such is not the case.

Therefore, my friend's question was far more concerned with the evolution of the human spirit and the maturing of the even deeper reality of the soul. It had little to do with identifying some mysterious purpose planted in our DNA at conception. His question could not be addressed, much less answered, by some half-baked, psycho/theological theory regarding the divine assignment of a specific pre-birth mission to each individual's life.

Again, I did not happen right away upon a satisfactory answer to my friend's searing inquiry into my work as a minister, at least not as I reviewed the first ten years or so of service to God through the church. Perhaps because this brief tenure proved to be an abusive and even, at times, toxic experience not only for me but for my family as well.

Following that arduous decade of service, the senior pastor who had invited me to join his staff, retired, thus leaving my colleagues and me in an awkward position. We were expected to resign and thereby allow our new, very young senior pastor the privilege of assembling his own staff.

There was just one problem with this protocol. None of us had any prospects whatsoever for any future employment. We all were stuck in an untenable situation where from time to time church leaders took us aside one by one to remind us of our obligation to resign.

At first, I did the only thing I could. I trusted God and resolved to be the best associate pastor possible, and I also decided to live one day at a time. This strategy worked until the new senior pastor arrived on the scene. He was a young, extraordinarily gifted and woefully inexperienced former seminary professor who let it be known to the church elders that he would, of course, prefer to assemble his own staff. Who could blame him? Had I been in his shoes, I would have done the same thing.

Secretly I hoped that this man would recognize my value as the pastor who had established programs and ministries to the poorest of Dallas' poor, thus giving this venerated old church its reason to remain downtown. However, such was not to be: A month or so after the new pastor arrived, I sent my first-ever request to the church's personnel committee asking to be granted a three-month sabbatical to our synod's conference center just west of Kerrville, Texas, and fulfill the request of this institution's board by writing the official history of Presbyterian Mo-Ranch Assembly.

Secondly, I requested permission to accept Austin Presbyterian Theological Seminary's invitation to teach a new master's-level course in community ministry. This minor request required nothing more than changing my day off from Friday to Monday.

The Personnel Committee addressed both requests and, of course, rejected both outright. Because the new pastor joined the committee in vetoing these two wonderful opportunities, I knew that my days in that church were now numbered.

I carried on as best I could for the next three months as I watched my daughter and my wife join another Presbyterian Church. Frankly, I enjoyed the dissonance their courageous decision created within the new pastor's inner circle, and yet, because of their decision, I endured even more attacks and ambushes from the church's lay leadership.

Time and time again, these people reminded me of what I already knew all too well. It was way past time for me to leave.

Finally, on an unusually warm November morning, I met with the Personnel Committee for my annual evaluation. While I had dreaded this conversation for weeks, I was surprised, almost shocked, to discover these folks were all smiles, and, at least, seemed to be most pleased with me and with my work for the past 12 difficult months. To a man—no women served on the committee—they praised my contributions to the church, and I responded with nods and sighs as I vented a bit of the enormous tension that had welled in my soul for more than a year.

Eventually, one of the elders inquired regarding my plans for the coming year. His question was like giant softball dropping across the plate and ready to be slugged over the wall for a grand slam.

I drew sufficient breath for what now had to be said. With what I hoped was a knowing smile containing far more content than I would ever share with these men in any other circumstance, I said, "Oh, I plan to resign and somehow find some other kind of work. And, with your permission, of course, I would like to remain here fully engaged until May 31st of next year."

These men appeared far more relieved than surprised, and yet one chose to say, "May we ask what precipitated this decision?"

I was grateful to feel a strong, yet still strange, sense of calm embracing me. Mysteriously I felt the arms of my maternal grandmother holding me just as she had done, when as a pre-school child I had been terror-stricken by the wild thunderstorms that dipped down from Oklahoma on occasion to rumble above the leaky roof of her small North Texas house.

Now I scanned the room. A consensus signaling something between relief and compassion was etched upon every man's countenance.

Finally, I managed to utter, "Your decision to reject the only two requests I've ever made of any one in this church is unacceptable. It's no secret you want me to go, and now I am simply complying with your wish."

The new pastor rushed his words and suggested we conclude this meeting with prayer. Once he finished, I abandoned the room.

Later that spring, I left the church and rewarded myself with the gift of a much-needed sabbatical at Mo-Ranch, where in three weeks I wrote the official and first-ever history of that very special place. At the end of that month, I returned to Dallas and entered into a two-year clinical residency in pastoral counseling and psychotherapy.

And in those very intense two years, not a day passed that I did not question myself regarding not only the point of a career so wracked by pain, disappointment, and abuse, but even more my life, which at the time I viewed as pretty much a dismal failure.

Finally, I discovered that my disappointment with the

church was a blessing bestowed upon me to teach me how to forgive. What I didn't understand yet is that one cannot possibly claim to be a follower of Jesus without making forgiveness a top priority and even an uncomfortably frequent practice. Once I accepted the idea that the mistreatment I suffered was a blessing, the bitterness infecting my soul dissipated and I felt truly alive again for the first time in years.

Our family barely made it financially, but we did scrape by. We even managed to see to it that our daughter never went without anything she really needed.

Although a new peace seeped into my soul following my daily discipline of forgiving those who had hurt me so, I still found myself asking the question: So what is the point?

Now that I am retired and have some time available to pursue projects that have long interested me, I decided to search for some kind of satisfactory response to the question as to the point of human existence in this world.

Simply put, the questions seem to be these:

> Why are we here on planet Earth such a brief time before we die?

> What are we supposed to make of this life?

> What exactly are we to do with it?

> How do we not waste it?

All these serious questions have tormented humankind ever since people could quit merely surviving long enough to ponder such sweeping existential issues. In fact, for many people today, these issues must be addressed, if not answered, if they ever hope to know any lasting serenity in their lives.

In my twenty-five year career as a pastoral counselor, I have had such concerns presented to me countless times, and often with a palpable sense of urgency and even desperation.

The culture we have created and share is all too eager to supply answers for us. Indeed, the culture is quick to tell us we are here to do primarily one thing: win.

From the time we are encouraged to draw the most simplistic and often erroneous conclusions regarding the world as we experience it, we discover we are expected to win something or someone. If we have siblings, we learn from the outset to compete for our parents' affection. And in school we learn to compete with our peers for acceptance in the most prestigious social groups.

I recall in the first grade being placed in the slowest reading group, and even today I remember the humiliation in being designated a "dumb kid" while my best friends were all assigned to the fastest reading group.

This kind of social competition continued throughout my educational years. Much later in my school experience, my friends and I were not so much concerned about our academic rank as we were our social status.

In retrospect, this is not at all surprising because psychology has taught us that adolescents universally feel a deep—and in the main, unconscious—need to affiliate with that social group which will broker the highest measure of social status. For adolescents, achieving social status is most often what it means to win.

In both high school and college, I competed until I grew exhausted from this crazy game of seeking approval and acceptance from people I both admired and too often envied. At last, somewhere in my final two years of undergraduate work, I somehow discovered two truths:

All long I had been accepted by God.

What other people thought of me was not then and would never be any of my business.

Nevertheless, I also learned that what I thought about other people—and even more how I treated them—was, indeed, God's business. Only when I figured out that belonging to some prestigious group did nothing to define me was I able to give up the painful yearning to belong.

In the aftermath of this "awakening," I gave up competing with any one about much of anything. Instead, I focused my energy on my post-graduation plans, and even more, on my spiritual life.

My experience is not unique, because we are all taught at a very early age to win something, whether it's affection, status, or some more tangible prize. For the majority of us, competition both defines and drives childhood and adolescence. Thus our earliest experiences teach us to chase after three false gods: status, success, however we define it, and image (or reputation). And for the majority of us, these powerful false gods torment us and yet relentlessly drive our decisions way past the mid-point in our lives.

While contemplating this chapter, I found myself snarled in a typical Austin, Texas, traffic jam. This congestion consisted of at least a dozen automobiles and one high-dollar van with a hand-painted sign emblazoned on the back window: "Stanford

Bound."

Because I was stuck in traffic, I permitted myself to ponder the implications of such a public display of some local family's obvious pride. My initial thought was to be proud of whatever young person in a local prestigious high school had gained admission to one of this nation's finest universities.

However, before any genuine celebrative thoughts could fill my mind, I next found myself wondering why anyone would feel compelled to proclaim such an accomplishment on the back window of the family van. I decided the sign was actually no different from those ubiquitous bumper stickers that read: "My child is an honor student at such and such a school."

Upon further reflection, I also decided that what the Stanford sign actually proclaimed was that the kid, who had gained admission to Stanford, had played the old competition game well and had definitely won. "We're big-time winners!" was the underlying message and true meaning of the sign, and sadly the majority of us are no different from the temporarily proud sign bearer.

As human beings we compete, and we compete to win. If we're honest with ourselves and with God, we will admit that we would much, much rather compete to win than surrender to God's Holy will. By our own intention we cannot become meek and thereby choose to be a loving soul, as opposed to playing the old familiar competition games.

Because of how our culture shapes us from the very beginning, we far more identify with legendary football coach Vince Lombardi's creed—"Winning isn't everything. It's the only thing."—than we do with most anything Jesus taught about loving our neighbor as we love ourselves, turning the other cheek, and even praying for those who persecute us.

In fact, the Gospel Jesus came to proclaim is so counterintuitive, so counter cultural and so radical as to cause even the most sincere Christians to miss altogether its core message. No, the majority of us Christians sit in the glow of stain glass sanctuaries and listen to sermons Sunday after Sunday without once pausing to realize that our real gods are the idols of success, status, and image.

Sadly, we profess Jesus as our Lord, while, in truth, we are much like the Children of Israel who worshiped the Golden Calf out there in the Sinai Peninsula three thousand years ago. We give some serious lip service to Jesus, and yet, all the while we worship at the throne of the unholy trinity of success, status, and image.

When I began this search, I was not sure where it would take me, but I long ago had embraced Sigmund Freud's and Soren Kierkegaard's idea that all real truth may only be discovered. Therefore I decided for an experiential approach, which meant one thing: introspection predicated upon my subjective, and likely too often myopic, view of Scripture. I knew of no one theologian or of even one universally respected clinician or philosopher whom I considered sufficiently wise or learned to answer to my satisfaction, at least, the question as to the purpose of human existence.

Over the past 40 years, I have known—and in some cases even befriended—several greatly respected theologians in both the Protestant and Catholic traditions. But as brilliant and as admired as these men and women are, none of them appeared capable of convincing me they could answer this question.

No, I realized that, like all people, I would have to discover the truth for myself. Furthermore, whatever I did discover could not be my truth until I finally bumped into it and accepted it, because, like it or not, truth is invariably subjective and always highly personal.

After no small amount of consideration my search carried me back to my roots and to one evening in particular in the summer of my 10th year when I was helping my beloved grand-daddy milk his small herd of cows by hand in his milking pen. Once finished, he and I rose at the same time from the three-legged stools we used, and Granddaddy handed me a full pail of warm milk before bewildering me with his latest expression of wisdom. "You know, Bobby, you can't never sit on no two-legged stool. It has to have three legs or it'll tip over every time."

If I responded, it was likely with nothing more than a shrug followed by a grunt. I carried that full pail of warm milk to the house and handed it to my grandmother, who later churned a portion of it into arguably the best-tasting butter in the universe.

However, I will never forget this adage the meaning of which was lost on me until I arrived at the seminary some 13 years later. During the course of studying Greek over the summer of 1970, I was given the assignment to translate Mark 12:28-32 from Greek into English. Determined to get this work done before sundown, I headed straight to the seminary's library, and I set about to discover the meaning of this text, which until some moments later was still very much Greek to me.

The following is my translation of that sacred text (with more than a little help from *The Revised Standard Version of the English Bible*):

"One of the scribes came near and heard them disputing with one another, and seeing that he answered them well, he asked him, "Which commandment is the first of all?"

Jesus answered, 'Hear, O Israel: The Lord our God, the Lord

is one; you shall love the Lord your God with all your heart and with all your soul, and with all your mind, and with all your strength. The second is this, "You shall love your neighbor as yourself."

After finishing the translation of this first verse, I rose from the rickety old library chair and descended the stairs toward the exit at the front entrance. I followed the sidewalk until I arrived at the curb of the street separating the seminary from the University of Texas campus. Sitting there alone in the shade of an ancient live oak tree, I realized that in this passage I had quite likely discovered my grandfather's three-legged stool.

As I saw it, the first leg is our absolute commitment to God or as Jesus put it, to "love God with all of our heart, soul, mind and strength." What this means is that we are to dedicate every part of us, both known and hidden, to a God, whose identity is pure love. More succinctly, we are to dedicate the whole of our very beings to the greatest Power in the universe, which, again, is love.

As I returned to my study carrel in the library, I discerned that these holy words from Mark's Gospel were likely the most powerful words my young mind had ever encountered and the most beautiful concept I've ever been invited to ponder. There it was: the key to happiness, the very foundation of sanity, the simple, but profound, blueprint for making life work, and most of all, the behavioral standard for what it means to claim citizenship in the Kingdom Jesus proclaimed.

So, the first leg of the three-legged stool is to love God with everything in us. Jesus tells us that the love he has in mind is the total devotion of one's mind, soul, heart, and strength to God as opposed to bowing our heads in prayer occasionally and dropping a dollar or two in the church offering plate every so often.

Rather, what Jesus has in mind is a total devotion to a life both defined by and also driven by divine love. Jesus knew that when we make such a commitment, we choose a life of holiness as opposed to a life both defined and driven by self-interest. Choosing to live a life devoted to loving God, others, and ourselves not only puts us at odds with a world dedicated to self-interest, it also makes us vulnerable to the myriad temptations of such a world. This more than any other reason is why we choose to be nominally religious rather than to become devoted followers of Jesus.

The second leg on the stool is the appropriate love of one's self. In my role as a pastoral counselor for twenty-five years, I've become convinced that loving one's self appropriately is, at best, a daunting challenge, and, at worse, an impossible dream for many people, especially those who were abused as children.

Long ago an elderly gentleman named Andy shared with me an illustrative and memorable story. This man, a former college president of a church-related school, had invested much of his time in his retirement years teaching the Bible to inmates in the Texas Department of Corrections.

On one particular evening, an inmate named Ray requested the opportunity to visit with him following class. Andy consented and, following the closing prayer, Ray shuffled his weight from foot to foot as if something had made him uncomfortable.

Andy invited Ray to sit next to him, and without hesitating Ray told his teacher he was concerned about himself. Intrigued by even such an obtuse observation, Andy encouraged Ray to continue.

"Last week I returned to my cell following my work in the

prison farm's fields, and I was surprised to find my cellmate in his bunk lying flat on his belly, face down, with his head covered by his pillow. At first, I thought he was sleeping, but then I heard him crying. I lifted the pillow from his head and I asked him why he was crying.

"He sat up and told me his mother had died and he couldn't go to her funeral because, of course, he was locked up. And that's when it happened. I had a good thought. For the first time in my life, I had a good thought.

"And that's what concerns me. So I patted my cellmate on the shoulder and told him how sorry I was for him. I've never been kind to any one before. And that is what really bothers me. What's happening to me, Andy?"

Andy smiled as he clasped the inmate on his shoulder. "Ray, I suspect God's been working on you. And you're beginning to love yourself enough to care about someone else. And that's a wonderful blessing."

Ray was in the earliest stages of what Jesus called being "born again." But because overuse and misunderstanding have so long corrupted this term, I now prefer "spiritually awakened."

Although he did not know it, Ray was dying to the old narcissistic, self-defeating, sociopathic self he had long ago created and was slowly, but inexorably, becoming the new, true self created by God in God's own holy image. And because this new self is of God and about God, it can only be about one thing: love.

This new self is also called the true self, and I name it this because from the very beginning all of us are made in the image of love, and, therefore, made for love and made to express love. But unfortunately, this fallen world so wounds us when we are young, we necessarily develop a constellation of ego defenses, the sum of which too often turn us into self-absorbed adults who find if difficult to love ourselves in the way Jesus intended.

Over my career, I've even worked with adults who are so wounded they claim it impossible to love themselves. I once offered counseling to a self-proclaimed marquee attorney who was trapped in a narcissistic personality disorder. In childhood he learned to equate self-love with the constant and wholly unrealistic praise his parents lavished upon him.

Before he could even graduate from high school, they had convinced him he was the smartest young man in the world whom God had chosen for true greatness. In his mind, he was the smartest, most handsome, athletic, charismatic, and charming young man on the planet.

He was, in fact, uncommonly gifted, but when he arrived on the campus of a large university, he faced some pretty stiff competition in every area of endeavor. This head-on collision with reality caused him to turn up the dial on his efforts for achieving status, and not surprisingly, he arrived in my office as a fifty-something, burned-out shell of a man whose inhumane work ethic had achieved for him a pile of money, notoriety, and legendary success. But it had also cost him two heart attacks, one marriage, and what appeared to be a permanent alienation from his children.

The moment I introduced the concept of self-love to him, he protested in a loud voice that he had no idea whatsoever what I was talking about. As I arose from my chair to draw the metaphorical model of the three-legged milking stool on the grease board affixed to my office wall, he stood up.

Before I could say anything else, he bolted through the office door and into the hallway. When I called to him, he turned and yelled in an angry tone, "Sorry, but I don't think you can help me, because I don't want to hear you to talk about God again!" And with that he flipped me off as he hurried down the hallway.

Unfortunately for him, in his own mind, God had had been reduced to the idols of success, status, and image. He had, over the course of his life, created himself in the image of his own pantheon of demanding little gods.

And precious few people are willing to abandon the gods of their own creation in favor of surrendering their lives to the God who created them in His holy image for the reconciling and noble purposes of a selfless love. Unless or until this man discovers and embraces the truth that he has been made in the image of unadulterated, unconditional love, he will most likely never know what it means to love himself appropriately.

Far too many people go through the whole of their lives trapped in the compulsive patterns of some unrealistic and fixed destructive belief system. Its attendant behaviors wear them out until it finally kills them in the unholy cause of seeking to please the unreasonable standards of the gods they have created.

This kind of existence knows nothing of the true God, who is perfect love, and therefore, it disallows the discovery of the true self, who is, of course, our individually unique expression of imperfect love. Today, many Christians find themselves in this conundrum, and with tragic consequences, and this kind of sick thinking is all too often blessed and perpetuated by those who preach the so-called "prosperity gospel."

God never commands us to be successful. But don't try to peddle that idea to Christians who in today's mega-churches have convinced themselves that God wants them to be wealthy and that their particular church needs to be the biggest, the richest, the most beautiful, and the most appealing cathedral in their city.

As I stated at the outset of this book, we human beings learn early on to be competitive, and sadly this is so even in our religious lives. Of course, preachers want bigger churches, because more people in the pews usually translate into larger salaries for themselves. Congregants want to belong to bigger churches because in America, it's inarguably axiomatic that bigger is invariably better, and bigger seems to garner prestige the way pigs draw flies.

But if we are to believe the Scripture, God doesn't want big, beautiful, and impressive temples. God wants loving, faithful, serving, and redemptive churches where people can come to worship and develop a personal relationship with God and with fellow sojourners. This new relationship will be one that fosters the discovery of the true self as a reflection of the one very God who is the object of their worship. To become the true self, then, is tantamount to loving one's self in a manner that is healthy, invariably redemptive, and always of God.

Keep in mind that Matthew's Gospel has Jesus telling us (in paraphrase) that where two or three are gathered in his name, there he will be there also. What none of the Gospels proclaims is that God requires, or for that matter even enjoys, thousands being gathered in his name.

The third leg of the stool is to love one's neighbor as you love yourself. This is only possible in us flawed human beings if we first embrace the universal truth that God loves us and accepts us, even when we are broken down and so full of shame, we can't lift our heads high enough to get our chins off our chests. The mysterious power that offers us love even when we know our own unworthiness is called grace.

For years I've heard pew-sitting people claim that there are no requirements for receiving grace. "We can't earn it," they say, and likewise, "We cannot possibly be good enough for God to bestow it on us."

And that is all true.

However, the one requirement of grace is, we must be willing to receive it. We must be willing to allow it to wash over us like the waters of our baptism so it might change us from self-serving and self-directed petty idolaters and into people who truly know what it means to love other people without strings and without the usual conditions that plague most human relationships.

Many years ago, I worked with an extraordinarily gifted colleague, who was one of the most insightful preachers and dynamic Bible teachers I'd ever encountered. His Monday night Bible classes were standing-room-only affairs in the mega church where we served together at the time. And when he preached, women swooned and grown men wept. What I appreciated most about him was the way he made grace the cornerstone of every sermon and Bible lesson.

After working with this gifted man for a full year, I was shocked to learn the church's leadership discovered he and another colleague had managed to embezzle approximately sixty-five thousand dollars from the church. This man possessed gifts that placed him in a role of authority before thousands, and, with an eloquence and passion I've seldom experienced in any one, he spoke of God's love and of the very kingdom for which Jesus so willingly died. Needless to say, this man was a phony and, at best, a con man who preyed upon the innocent in order to steal their money as well as their hearts.

Of course, he is an extreme example of counterfeit spirituality, and he is not the kind of man I want loving me as he loves himself. If this man ever had decided to love me as he loved himself, I might well have ended up precisely where he did. In jail.

I reference him only because he is a grotesque image of the condition in which most of us Christians find ourselves mired. We may not be con men or thieves, but all too often, like him, our thinking and our lives do not line up with what it means to love God, and to love our neighbors as ourselves.

We profess a faith we do not dare live out. This also means we must clean up our spiritual lives if we ever hope to be able to love ourselves or any one else, including God.

During my tenure in Dallas, I sought to purchase a derelict apartment house, renovate it, and then offer it rent-free to homeless families until they could get on their feet. A leader in the church approached me with an offer to sell the church the apartment complex he owned in South Dallas.

I had no idea he owned such a property, so I shook his hand and agreed to accompany him to the site in order to see if it might serve our needs for establishing a housing ministry in Dallas. We met for a pleasant lunch in a fine downtown restaurant before venturing in his stylish automobile to a black neighborhood in the shadow of Dallas' iconic old Cotton Bowl. The afternoon was fast turning stifling with the temperature soaring above the century mark and with the humidity challenging long-standing records.

When we arrived at the front steps, I was shocked at the poor condition of this so-called complex. The place appeared uninhabitable and in need of the city's immediate condemnation. The cracks in the exterior walls were so pronounced, I was certain the foundation had long since moved to a different address far down the block. I knew, even before asking, that this building was not equipped with any kind of air conditioning, and yet every window on both floors remained shut, thus making it next to impossible to breathe on the inside on the miserably hot Dallas August afternoon of our visit.

"How could anyone possibly claim ownership of such a dump?" I asked myself as I followed him into the first apartment.

Just as I expected, the interior was even hotter than outside. A stream of raw sewage leaked from an upstairs bathroom and ran down a plaster wall and into the living room where this church elder and I now stood. The stench was not only sickening, but I suspected also hazardous to my health. Trying not to appear too nauseated, I informed the man I'd seen enough and he led me again outside and into the fresh, but still hot, air.

We remained silent on our return trip to my office at the church. I recall staring out the car window at the passing scene, all the while dazed not so much by the heat and the stench as by the realization that one of the key leaders in our church was a slumlord.

This man had been granted authority to help govern the church, and yet I had just discovered something about his character that made me wonder if his heart, mind, and soul were not oblivious to the suffering of his fellow human beings.

How could he not know that being a slumlord is tantamount to slavery? How could he not have heard the Gospel of love and liberation my colleagues and I had preached to him for years? How could he remain so insensitive to and so detached from the suffering of others? How could he not raze this eyesore and replace it with the kind of new and sturdy edifice that fostered a sense of security and comfort in those who occupied it?

Once more Matthew's Gospel informs my questions, by having Jesus pose a question of his own: "Why do you seek the speck in your neighbor's eye, but do not notice the log in your own eye?" (Matt. 7:3)

What this means is that I cannot point to this man's sin of operating such an enterprise without first falling into the trap of becoming a finger-wagging, chest-thumping Pharisee myself. Since I don't wish to assume that role any more than I already have, I will move on by declaring the truth that this man's sins are very likely no worse than my own.

But the real point of telling this story is to suggest that simply belonging to and even being active in a church is not enough. We can claim to be a Christian and still not know Jesus. We can recite the creeds, pray the prayers, sing the songs, and hear the sermons and still not have a clue as to what it means to follow Jesus.

During my decade of founding programs for the homeless and the helpless of Dallas, I was surprised to encounter so little resistance in creating spaces where the homeless and the vulnerable might feel safe and might experience the love of Jesus Christ made palpable. However, the one big exception was the strong, even at times, ugly resistance I received from the very church I served. While the pastors were unified in their support of the founding of the soup kitchen, the lay leadership was not. Again and again, folks repeated, "Why are we inviting bums and winos into our church when what we really need to do is to attract wealth?"

As a young and terribly naïve recent seminary graduate, I was saddened by the church's initial resistance. How could people, many of whom claimed to be born again Christians, oppose the very core teachings of their Lord?

At first, a few threatened to shut us down. But as time passed, the people of Dallas deemed the soup kitchen a good thing and contributed money to it with such generosity as to guarantee its future for years to come. I am thankful it still operates on a daily basis and is an ecumenical ministry supported by Episcopal, Methodist, and Jewish congregations. As I write this book, this ministry has celebrated more than four decades of service to the homeless of Dallas.

CHAPTER 2

Awakenings

Sometime during the early years of operating a Dallas soup kitchen, which was nothing more than a converted basement parking garage, I met Harry. As I stood guard at the entrance one bitterly cold January morning, he attempted to bull his way into our dining room, drawn by the relative warmth from our one big suspended space heater. Harry was young, strong, and so stumbling drunk there was no way I could allow him into our otherwise peaceful shelter.

About ninety-nine per cent of our regulars always hovered somewhere between drunk and hung over. I knew them from years of association, and most of them were harmless old street characters who would have collapsed from exhaustion after missing me with their first swing.

What neither Harry nor I could know on the morning of my refusal to practice Christian charity and hospitality was that, in this soup kitchen, Harry's life would become forever changed. But nothing spectacular was to happen to Harry on this particular day, because he was far too drunk, far too big, far too angry, and just about far too everything else to be admitted.

Right away I stepped in front of him. I did my best to prevent him from becoming so violent as to cause the church to shut this ministry down forever. A few patrons had already gathered at the tables to assuage their standard morning hangovers with a cup or two of hot coffee.

Just as my colleague and Episcopal street priest Fr. Jerry Hill had taught me, I reached for a broom I kept stationed at the entrance. With the broomstick gripped in my hands, I said to him in a polite tone, "Sir, you are not welcome here today because you're too drunk. When you are sober, you will be most welcome."

This big man now glared at me with the fires of some ancient rage smoldering in his eyes. As I placed the broom in front of me in a defensive position, he spit at least a morning's worth of cheap wine and saliva onto the icy sidewalk. With both fists clinched, he screamed loud enough to silence all conversation in the dining room, as well as to summon support from some of the volunteer staff.

What little wine and spit remained in his mouth now attached themselves to his angry words and landed upon my face. "And I'm going to kick your ass, mister!"

Fortunately Harry's mood quickly changed from resentment to resignation. With a sigh of relief, I watched him meander his way down the sidewalk toward the Farmer's Market where I suspected he managed to beg or steal sufficient sustenance to carry him into the next day.

A day or so later, we admitted a far more sober version of Harry to the soup kitchen, and over the next couple of years he became a compliant, and even grateful, regular who kept to himself and caused no problems. He ate his daily meal of a bowl of free vegetable beef stew, cornbread, and cold milk, and then departed as quietly as he had entered.

Over time I even grew to like him enough to enjoy an occasional morning conversation over coffee where I found him to be intelligent, surprisingly literate, and articulate. His spirit was gentle, except when contaminated by two-dollar wine, and his demeanor was, for the most part, serene. He possessed a sensitivity that made me wonder if he had been so wounded, and perhaps, even so broken by life that he had given up on himself and then sought refuge in the existential purgatory that is street life.

I possessed no real information on Harry because, out of respect for his privacy, I never chose to probe. Nevertheless, I did often wonder what we in the church might do for one so capable and still so young. I viewed it as a sin to allow our passivity to collude with his slow strategy for slow, agonizing self-destruction. Still, I reminded myself often that I had no right whatsoever to impose my positive perceptions of Harry upon the tragic reality of his need to self-destruct.

However, all of that changed the day Billy, a notorious old street character, tapped on the door of my office to report that Harry had succeeded in killing himself and that his body lay under a derelict ice house in a South Dallas ghetto less than two miles from the church. Father Jerry Hill, my beloved colleague, and I drove the church van to the icehouse where we discovered Harry still alive, but dangerously sick from alcohol poisoning and various other disorders. We took gentle care to remove him from beneath the abandoned building and drove him to Parkland Hospital, Dallas County's charity hospital. Once there, we turned him over to the medical personnel before returning to the church.

Six weeks or so later, a sheepish Harry tapped on my office door and asked if he might be invited in. He appeared to be a very different man from the tough street drunk I'd first encountered at the soup kitchen's entrance several years before. This man looked gaunt, at least 50 pounds lighter, obviously humble, and visibly whipped.

I trembled as I studied his appearance and considered the reasons underlying his unexpected presence at my office door. Of course, I invited him in and pointed toward a chair. With the kind of sigh that is born only of some kind of deep suffering, Harry eased his long, thin body into the chair and waited for me to speak. Once the amenities were out of the way, Harry shared the following story.

First he told me what I already knew. He had remained in Parkland for the past few weeks. And one night while he was on the drunk ward drying out, something happened.

He then paused long enough to study my face for clues of any possible response. Harry must have read in my smile and my countenance sufficient reassurance to continue.

He told me a light had come to him in that room and had spoken to him, saying he could live or he could die. The light further told him the choice lay entirely with him. He told the light he wanted to live and it disappeared.

With more anguish than should ever be etched upon any one man's face, Harry said, " What happened to me, Bob? What happened to me?"

"I suspect you were visited by a messenger from God, Harry."

"Like maybe some kind of angel?"

"Perhaps."

Harry's sigh was deeper than any words he could possibly offer, and following the silence between us that ensued, he departed my office and, for the most part disappeared both from my presence and from my mind.

However, a decade or so after I moved from Dallas to Austin to begin a new life, Harry's wife called me. She invited me back to Dallas for Harry's presentation to the bishop of that region's Episcopal diocese. Harry was to be ordained a deacon in the Episcopal Church and he had requested I be a part of his ordination service and share in his joy.

Immediately, I hung up the phone, rose from my chair, and walked outside and into the first light of that new morning. Once alone, I hoped a new breeze might carry my simple utterances of thanksgiving all the way to Heaven.

When I arrived in Dallas for the ordination, I learned a good bit more about Harry: Not only had he gotten married to a faithful soup kitchen volunteer, but he had also been appointed as the executive director of the homeless shelter Fr. Hill and I had founded years before. In addition, he earned a college degree, had become a licensed alcohol and drug counselor, and was credited with starting several AA groups among the homeless of downtown Dallas.

Somehow by the great mystery that is grace, Harry had been awakened to embrace to the fullest his true identity. He had thus been transformed from a wreck of a human being, who only lived to die, into an extraordinarily loving man. He only wished to serve the God who had saved him from himself.

Tears welled in my eyes, as Harry, newly ordained, served me a cup of communion wine---the very substance he had used in the attempt to kill himself years before he encountered Christ in a soup kitchen.

* * *

Grapeland, Texas, is the quintessence of a small southern town. In some ways it could be an inspiration for one of Norman Rockwell's illustrations of pure Americana. However, in other ways, its very existence serves as a reminder of a much darker era when strict Jim Crow Laws were the unquestioned norm. This is perhaps most evident in the living conditions of the town's black residents.

Grapeland was never large enough to be considered for the county seat, but it did serve as a sleepy commercial hub for the peanut farmers and the cotton growers who depended upon it for such necessities as light bread and gasoline. It was big enough to support a few stores, all of which were lined up on one side of the street, along with a couple of small industries that somehow managed to survive even hard times. But it was never big enough to be considered of much importance by anyone outside the bounds of Houston County, one of the poorest, if not the poorest, county in Texas.

My father, who was raised on tenant farms about ten miles or so from Grapeland, attended its public schools and throughout all those years he dreamed of escaping not only the poverty, but also the prejudice and rigid social "caste system" that formed the cultural fabric of his childhood.

The Grapeland I came to know in frequent visits to my grandparents' farm was still segregated, with the black people living in what was then a collection of shacks known as "the Quarter."

The single business in the Quarter was a ramshackle store where folks might buy a can of something if, that is, the something they sought happened to be in stock. In addition, there was an AME Church, which was not much bigger than any spacious living room on the white side of town and a small structurally challenged school that housed all twelve grades and in good years might be staffed by two teachers.

I often rode with my grandfather into the Quarter on Saturday mornings where I watched him peddle sweet milk, buttermilk, butter, and produce to folks who had come to trust him and to view him as a man of uncommon integrity. By the time I was old enough to begin my college career, I had come to regard this primitive sad collection of shacks as one of the final vestiges of the egregious racial sins of the old South. And I wondered if anything good or anyone extraordinary might rise above the deprivations that formed such places as the Quarter.

A few years ago, I happened upon a story in the Austin paper about a 17 year-old kid from Grapeland named Napoleon Beazley. Napoleon Beazley was an honor student, football star, class president, and the son of one of the most prominent black families in Grapeland. Napoleon Beazley would have been one of the brightest stars ever produced by the Grapeland ISD, except for one thing. He committed a murder.

On April 9, 1994, Napoleon Beazley and two friends, the Coleman brothers, drove two hours to the city of Tyler, Texas. Once there, he and his friends spotted a white Mercedes Benz sharing the same slow flow of traffic. Right away, the three young men from Grapeland decided they wanted to take possession of the Mercedes.

They followed the car even as it turned into the driveway of a suburban residence. Napoleon jumped from his car and approached the Mercedes on foot. As the driver of the Mercedes exited the car, Napoleon Beazley placed the barrel of a .38-caliber handgun to the man's head and squeezed the trigger, killing the car's driver, a much respected and beloved retiree.

Of course, in time Napoleon Beazley was arrested and first

charged with and later convicted of murder in the first degree. The death sentence was to be his fate for several reasons:

> (1) in Texas judges and juries hand out death sentences the way generous suburbanites distribute candy on Halloween night;

> (2) the crime was "cold blooded," or, that is, premeditated;

> (3) this was a black-on-white crime, and in Texas a disproportionate number of blacks sit on Death Row; and finally,

> (4) Texans love the death penalty.

In fact, Texas houses more in-mates on Death Row and executes more convicts than any other state or even any other country in the world. Since Governor Ann Richards held office, no man or woman since has ever been—or could ever be—elected governor in Texas without being a strong and vocal proponent of the death penalty.

Napoleon Beazley languished on Death Row for close to a year before being executed by lethal injection at the age of 18. The night of his execution, I drove from my home into downtown Austin where I parked my car on Lavaca Street about a half mile from the Governor's mansion.

The early spring evening was still warm and muggy as it portended the coming blast furnace that is summer in Central Texas. To be honest, I didn't know why I walked toward the Governor's Mansion except that I knew I needed to do something. But what?

Of course, I recognized my chilling powerlessness in this excruciating moment; nevertheless I remained on the curb in the shadow of the Texas Governor's Mansion, where inside a politician, with presidential aspirations—and thus an image to uphold—held another man's life and death in his hands, just as did Pontius Pilate two-thousand years before.

But in this case the young man from Grapeland was in no way innocent. Napoleon Beazley had definitely committed this heinous murder in cold blood, and, in the eyes of the law, he had to be punished.

There was no real question here except, of course, for the moral question of capital punishment itself: Was killing Napoleon Beazley morally right?

In that Jesus Christ was the victim of state-sanctioned capital punishment, I've always thought it impossible to accept that God blesses our killing of our fellow human beings in the ill-conceived and unfounded theory that state-sanctioned homicide somehow deters murder. I agree with the parsimonious capital punishment protest placards that read: "Stop the killing of people to stop the killing of people."

There behind the Governor's Mansion, I questioned my motives as I fought off the impulse to bolt. I felt silly as I viewed my one-man silent protest as a meek, and altogether impotent, whisper in opposition to a massive and well-lubricated killing machine that couldn't be stopped.

I jaywalked across Lavaca Street until I reached the curb opposite the Mansion. Sitting on the curb, I bowed my head not to pray so much as to examine my motives.

Was I there because I believed Napoleon Beazley to be innocent? No.

Was I there because of my nostalgic link to his hometown of Grapeland? Possibly.

Was I there because I believe the death penalty is every bit as opposed to God as what Napoleon Beazley did in Tyler one year earlier? Absolutely.

Feeling now somewhat comforted by my renewed resolve to see the death penalty forever banned in Texas, I lifted my eyes to see an elderly woman walking toward my place on the curb. She wore the kind of smile that signals friendliness and a tee shirt that proclaimed her membership in some local United Methodist Church. In her hand she carried a hand-painted placard that read: "Don't kill for me!"

I liked her right off, but if we entered into any conversation, I've forgotten what we said. However, what I do recall is experiencing the overwhelming urge to pray, and perhaps that is because I felt so powerless sitting there on an Austin curb next to an old woman holding a single sign of protest.

In that moment I recalled a seminary professor proclaiming these three words: "Prayer is power!"

Perhaps it is. Nevertheless, I still felt somewhat ridiculous as I bowed my head to pray for the governor to have mercy just this one time and stay the execution of an 18 year-old boy who must have been under the influence of something evil, be it a toxic chemical, peer pressure, or some other worldly dark power, that night in Tyler.

Although I heartily agreed with professor's convictions regarding the power of prayer, I recognized that my words would likely change nothing except, perhaps, alter my emotional state from despair to a more bearable resignation. As the sun set, I rose from the curb, bid the woman farewell, and walked toward the place where an hour or so before I had parked my car.

Napoleon Beazley was dead before I arrived at my home some ten or so miles from the Governor's Mansion.

Only moments before the people of Texas put Napoleon Beazley to death, he spoke his final words recorded below. As you read these words, ponder their profundity and ask yourself if these words came from the mind of a cold-blooded killer or rather from the awakened soul of a young man who now knew God in a way precious few people ever do.

"The act I committed to put me here was not just heinous, it was senseless. But the person who committed that act is no longer here—I am. I'm not going to shout, use profanity, or make idle threats. Understand, though, that I'm not only upset, but I'm saddened by what is happening here tonight. I'm not only saddened, but also disappointed that a system that is supposed to protect what is right and just can be so much like me when I made the same shameful mistake. If someone tried to dispose of everyone here for participating in this killing, I'd scream a resounding 'No.'

"I'd tell them to give all of them the gift they would not give me... and that's to give them a second chance. I'm sorry I'm here. I'm sorry you're all here. I'm sorry John Luttig died. And I'm sorry it was something in me that caused all this to happen to begin with.

"Tonight we tell the world there are no second chances in the eyes of justice. Tonight we tell our children that in some instances, some cases, killing is right. This conflict hurts us all; there are no sides.

"The people who support this proceeding think this is justice. The people who think I should live think that is justice. As difficult as it may seem, this is a clash of ideals, with both parties committed to what they feel is right. But who's wrong, if in the end, we're all victims? In my heart I have to believe there is a peaceful compromise to our ideals. I don't mind if there are none for me, as long as there are for those who are yet to come. There are a lot of men like me on death row—good men—who fell to the same misguided emotions, but may not have recovered as I have. Give those men a chance to do what's right. Give them a chance to undo their wrongs. A lot of them want to fix the mess they started, but don't know how. The problem is not that people aren't willing to help them find out, but the system is telling them it won't matter anyway.

"No one wins tonight. No one gets closure. No one walks away victorious."

(Texas Dept. of Corrections public database.)

* * *

Of course, the most vivid example from history of an awakened soul is that of a man named Saul who hailed from the ancient city of Tarsus in what is today Turkey. This genius was so uncomfortable in his own skin, by convenience and without awareness, he made his religion his god. Saul was not only obsessed with his religion but also fixated on the twisted idea of making himself feel secure by seeing to it that everyone viewed God through the same subjective prism he employed.

Scripture teaches that Paul was a bystander who approved of the stoning of Stephen, one of the first men in the post-resurrection period to proclaim Jesus as the Christ in public. But Saul was much more than a bystander. He was a willing participant in the persecution of those early believers in Jesus Christ, who were then called "the people of the way."

St. Luke writes in his Acts of the Apostles (chapter 9:1-2): "Meanwhile Saul, still breathing threats and murder against the disciples, went to the high priest and asked him for letters to the synagogue at Damascus, so that if he found any who belonged to the Way, men or women, he might bring them bound to Jerusalem."

Again, at this point in his young life Saul is so insecure in himself and in his faith that he believes he must punish, even to the point of killing, those who appropriate God in a way different from his own. This is sociopathic! And a sociopath is one who willingly injures, or worse, kills someone with absolutely no remorse. We can be sure Saul had no remorse for the murder of Stephen, and neither would he have any remorse for those he thought needed killing once he reached Damascus.

I've met a few Pharisees in my 40-plus years of pastoral ministry. None of those folks would likely have killed another human being, but some were quite willing to destroy the careers and foment chaos in the lives of those with whom they disagreed on a theological basis.

I will never forget being summoned to a meeting of the candidates' committee of my presbytery when I was within two months of graduating from seminary. As I entered the small meeting room in the basement of the seminary's administration building, I was quick to note an older man glowering at me through the narrow slits of his constant squint.

I very much wanted to quit looking at him, but I couldn't because he wore a really bad toupee. In fact, it was so bad it appeared as though a squirrel had died and fallen out of tree and landed sideways on the man's head. Of all the members of the committee, he alone rose to shake my hand as he told me what

I already knew. He was from a large fundamentalist, evangelical church in Dallas.

The meeting went well enough until the man under the bad toupee asked me if I thought people who were not Christian went to hell when they died.

Because I was young, a bit cocky, and naive in the ways of the church, I said, "Sir, I don't believe a loving God ever sends any soul to hell, but I do believe human beings send themselves and/or venture to hell every day. For example, I believe drug addiction is hell, as is any kind of uncontrollable compulsion. Alcoholism is hell and so is untreated anxiety and depression. Intense loneliness is hell as is any kind of serious mental illness—"

"So you don't believe God sends sinners to hell. Is that what you're saying?"

I continued, "Sir, I don't believe there is a literal hell except for the suffering people experience right here in this life."

The man seethed with rage. "Son, I will personally see to it that you are never ordained by this presbytery."

And with that the meeting concluded, I made as hasty an exit as possible back to the safety of the apartment my wife and I shared on the seminary campus.

This man was a modern-day Pharisee in that he was so wedded to his own belief system; he viewed any one holding a competing conviction as a genuine danger to the church. Furthermore, he viewed it as his ordained mission to protect the church from everyone who did not share his rigid literal view of scripture.

Years later I learned he had traveled about in Presbyterian circles in Dallas doing his best to convince people with power in the church to ban me forever from North Texas.

This kind of behavior reminds me a great deal of Saul of Tarsus on his way to Damascus. To be clear, this man never actually meant to kill me, but he was definitely hell-bent on killing a dream for which I had sacrificed much and worked hard to bring to fruition for the previous four years.

I have no idea if this man ever awakened from the fear that drove his life and kept him imprisoned in the self he had created and imagined he needed to defend with a rage born of self-righteousness. He never bothered to apologize, and I managed to escape his evil intent by accepting a job at a small liberal arts college in Arkansas, which was far beyond his frustrated grasp.

Saul of Tarsus, however, was knocked to the ground by a light that spoke to him this question: "Saul, Saul, why do you persecute me?" (Acts 9:4b)

Of course, we know from Luke's account in the Acts of the Apostles that in this dramatic moment, this man's feet were placed on a path very different from the one he first intended to follow once he reached Damascus. From that moment forward and for the remainder of his life, this man Saul, who later changed his name to Paul, lived his life in his true self.

For on the road to Damascus, Paul not only discovered that Jesus is the risen Christ, but he also discovered his true identity for the very first time in his life. Living in the false self for, perhaps as many as three decades, Saul was ever driven by fear and ruled only by a tyrannical ego.

But as Paul, he awakened to the amazing truth that, because he had been created in the image of God, his true identity was love and his purpose in this life was to become the living, breathing, flesh-and-blood expression of that love.

In his letter to the church at Galatia, Paul tells us that following his moment with Jesus on the road to Damascus, he spent three years in Arabia. While he doesn't reveal how he spent those three years, we can reasonably assume that as an intellectual he was accustomed to investing much of his energy and time to the disciplines of scholarship.

But what did he study? Pharisees spent their lives studying and even memorizing the law, and yet, if his brief conversation with Jesus on the road had taught him anything, it must have been that the truth of God's will was to be discovered in the life, death, and resurrection of Jesus Christ.

Although scripture does not inform us regarding the details of Paul's time in Arabia, my hunch is that he spent his days praying and allowing himself to die slowly, but inexorably, to the self he had made up so that he might be raised again in the new identity of who he truly had been from the very beginning. And for the remainder of his life prayer so informed his mind that he wrote letters that in time became holy scripture, he founded churches, and he forever shaped the whole of Western civilization by inventing the religion we call Christianity. Only Jesus Christ himself made a greater contribution to this world.

Paul's life illustrates the truth that love is by far the greatest power in this world, while the life of the man who sought to derail my ministry so many years ago proves only one thing.

Fear amounts to nothing.

CHAPTER 3

Love

As I tucked my four-year-old grandson into his little bed, I said, "Henry, who loves you?"

His answer was both reflexive and surprisingly profound. "Everybody," he said.

I chuckled as I knelt to place my hand on his head. "Henry, you are so right, because you are so loved by everyone who knows you." And with that, I kissed him on his forehead one last time and bid him a good night.

Like the rest of us, Henry cannot define love, but without question, he knows what it is. And he knows what it is because he's experienced it for the whole of his life as it has been offered to him by his family, his friends, his preschool teachers, and even by strangers touched by his precocious personality.

The reason Henry cannot define love is the same reason none of us can define it. Simply put, love is indefinable.

And why is that so? Because love is a mystery, and even more, it is the ultimate mystery in that love is God's core identity. And God insists upon remaining a mystery.

All love flows from God and comes only through us as we express it to ourselves, back to God, and also to others. As much as we like to believe the cultural notions about love being an almost uncontrollable emotion that possesses the power to sweep us off our feet and make us uproariously euphoric for a time, the authentic love that is expressed by the true self is not that at all.

So what is it? Love is not only the greatest power on Earth and at the same time an indefinable mystery; it is also the very purpose of our existence. Said another way: Love is the very point of our being, because God made us in his image, and therefore, for love.

The good news is that we don't need to define love in order to express it, because all authentic love is a person's conscious choice to live out certain disciplines. And these disciplines never originate in the emotions, but rather always in the conscious mind.

Love is always a conscious decision. The true self chooses to love in every situation because he or she has been awakened to the revelation that his or her identity reflects the far greater identity that is God.

In his first letter, St. John writes of our natural and inextricable relationship with love far better than I ever could:

> "Beloved, let us love one another, because love is from God; everyone who loves is born of God and knows God. Whoever does not love does not know God, for God is love."
>
> (First letter of John 4:7)

So what exactly are the disciplines of love? St. Paul, in the thirteenth chapter of his immortal first letter to the church at Corinth lists them. Again, love is an indefinable mystery; hence Paul never attempts to explain it. He merely lists love's characteristics, each of which I have come to view as a distinct discipline. And these disciplines are as follows:

1. Love is the discipline of patience.

2. Love is the discipline of being kind.

3. Love is the discipline of restraining one's self from being envious, or boastful, or arrogant, or rude.

4. Love is the discipline of both promoting and protecting another's freedom in that it does not insist upon its own way.

5. Love is the discipline of restraining one's self from negative emotions in that love is neither irritable nor resentful;

6. Love is the discipline of living only in the truth, and avoiding all wrongdoing no matter the extenuating circumstances that might appear to justify it. Living exclusively in the truth means, among other things, that rationalizations are a thing of the past.

Many brides have requested I read this thirteenth chapter of First Corinthians at their wedding ceremony, and, of course, I comply. However, I often find myself wondering just how seriously young couples take these words, because over half of the marriage ceremonies I conducted during the past four decades have ended in divorce.

Only those who have experienced a true spiritual awakening can hope to know what it means to love. The true self is not only willing, but even more, committed to living out daily the disciplines of love.

The false self is driven almost exclusively by this question:

"What in this current situation can benefit me?"

The true self, however, consciously asks and then lives this question:

"How can I best express love in this current situation?"

As far as I'm concerned, only two kinds of music exist: country and western, and I love both kinds. My car radio is permanently tuned to Austin's premier C&W station. What I appreciate most about this music is its simple honesty. The songs tell stories that are almost always mournful, sad, and rife with heartache.

And I've long believed the listening public enjoys this somber genre simply because it makes us all feel better to realize that our lives, although certainly imperfect, are not nearly as burdened with suffering as the circumstances portrayed in the radio songs.

As a retired pastoral counselor, what I find most interesting in the songs is their disparate takes on the great mystery that is love. The lyrics tell of people who fall so hard and so fast in love they never fully recover. Their lives are shattered, if not altogether destroyed. These songs not only tell of falling in love, but they also sometimes even tell of the strange phenomenon of falling out of love. Within this genre, love is portrayed as an external force over which the susceptible prove powerless. In some songs, this power is viewed as ecstasy, while in others, love is the fount of all misery.

Similar mischaracterizations of love come also from other forms of entertainment, such as movies, romance novels, and popular television series. No wonder we human beings are so confused by what it means to love. For the whole of our lives, we have been inundated with a flood of misinformation about the greatest mystery in the entire universe.

When I was an adolescent, I was just as confused as my peers about what it meant to love. Even though I dared to tell a couple of girlfriends I loved them, I had no idea whatsoever what it meant to love them or anyone else. Nevertheless, I spoke of love like I knew a great deal about it.

In all honesty, I seldom considered either love's requirements or its origin. I was blessed to grow up in a wonderful family where my parents loved my three brothers and me with such efficacy that we grew into men who today acknowledge openly and frequently just how fortunate we were to be loved for the whole of our lives.

The truth is that we were so loved we never really knew anything else. Consequently, we arrived into our adult lives convinced that love was both a given and a universal norm. In other words, we believed all sons and daughters everywhere were raised in a family that loved with the same power as our parents had demonstrated every day.

I didn't let go of this conviction until the day I entered a two-year full time counseling residency. In time I was inundated with all manner of hurting clients who had been so wounded in childhood they had no real palpable experience with love. Many of these people were more than a little reticent to speak of love, or even to hear the word, because the word love had been often used to manipulate them in a way that resulted in abuse.

For example, I recall the misguided and super-religious father who abandoned his prodigal teenage daughter to the streets of downtown Dallas at midnight in order to teach her to quit running away. As he dragged her out of the backseat of the family car and pushed her to the curb, he screamed, "I'm only doing this because I love you!"

As the sun rose the next morning, she staggered into our soup kitchen barely alive. Her face was bruised and bloody and what was once a dress had been ripped to shreds. One of our female volunteers assisted her to a chair where she held this girl in her lap while the child sobbed inconsolably.

Realizing her immediate needs were far beyond our limited capabilities, I called the police and requested an officer and an ambulance staffed with paramedics. These first responders arrived in minutes and right away both questioned and comforted the girl with medical attention. Once she was able to speak, she reported that during the night she had been gang raped three times by three different groups of homeless men.

Of course, her father never intended for her to be assaulted when he sought to teach her a lesson by dumping her on the streets of downtown Dallas. Nevertheless, his decision to act on his own perverse perceptions of love not only forever traumatized his young daughter, but also placed her very life in jeopardy.

As this tragic illustration demonstrates, it is so important that people make an earnest effort to learn what it means to truly love others.

On another occasion, I interrupted a rare Saturday morning meeting to attend to the obvious needs of a boy who wandered into the church seeking some kind of help. He smelled like a county garbage dump in August and was covered in so much grime it appeared he had not bathed in a month. I turned the meeting over to one of the church elders and excused myself so that I might at least hear this boy's story.

As the kid trailed behind me to my office, he spoke not a word. He only filled the hallway with the kind of sighs St. Paul wrote about. They are far too deep for words.

However, once seated on the garage sale sofa in my office, his words came in a rapid-fire pattern. In minutes I learned he had run away from his home in a small Colorado mountain town and that he was profoundly sorry for worrying his parents and for everything else. (I chose not inquire regarding what "everything else" involved. The details belonged where they lay, between him and his parents.) He further told me he wanted to go home, but he wasn't at all sure if he would be welcome.

I offered to call his parents for him. His smile emboldened me to request his home phone number.

I dialed the number and listened as a deep voice that sounded far more like a primal growl than a "Hello" answered. I introduced myself and told the deep voice the boy wanted to come home. I explained how desperate and dangerous his situation had become due to his poor decisions, and I next promised to put him on a Trailways bus bound for Denver at absolutely no cost to the family. I even passed on the boy's apology to what now sounded like a now dead line.

"Tell him we don't want him back. And tell him, that as far as we're concerned, he's dead."

I wanted to argue on the boy's behalf, but I had no authority to do so. With the receiver still pressed against my ear, I waited for the man to change his mind. With an unexpected anger tightening my face and gripping my gut, I remained silent.

Next, a woman's voice spoke into the phone. "But please tell him we love him."

"I can't tell him that, ma'am."

"And why not?"

"Because it's not the truth."

In that moment, my response was not at all loving, and I had no right whatsoever to be judgmental. But my angry and ugly false self has a way of surfacing in such moments, and I always regret its appearance and even more the unkind words it so thoughtlessly utters.

After hanging up, I located a twenty-dollar bill I kept stashed in my bottom desk drawer for just such emergencies, and I handed it to the boy.

Tears flooded his eyes. "They won't take me back?"

"No, they will not."

"So what do I do?

I gave him directions to our all-night shelter where he could linger all day Sunday with no questions asked. I explained he could shower and be fed there at no charge. Furthermore, I told him that he would be safe.

He took the money, shook my hand, and turned for the door, but tarried for a moment longer, seeming to want something more.

"Come back on Monday" I said, "when I have access to more funds and I can put you on a bus to some place not Dallas."

He exited the church in silence and disappeared into the glare and cacophony of downtown Dallas. I never saw him again.

So what does it really mean when we tell someone we love him or her? For me, it means I'm making a binding commitment to vouchsafe their freedom, even (and especially) from me, and in this commitment I promise to live out the disciplines listed above. Keep in mind we can only make and keep such a commitment out of the true self.

The false self cannot possibly make or keep this or any real commitment, because the false self is governed always by the well-defended and ever insatiable ego. And every needy ego is—by its very nature—anxious and therefore rejects by reflex any thought of allowing or, even more, protecting the freedom of those whom it purports to love.

I was once blessed to participate in a family's crisis that proved to serve as an unforgettable lesson in the power of authentic love to liberate a man from the darkness and to return him to the light.

One morning Fr. Hill and I sipped coffee at the soup kitchen entrance as we enjoyed the early spring sunshine warming our faces. All of a sudden Fr. Hill tossed his full Styrofoam cup straight up into the new morning as he began to sprint north on the sidewalk toward Jackson Street.

Because I had learned from experience that this man's instincts were always to be trusted, I also flung my cup to the sidewalk and joined this mad dash toward something or someone, I was not at all certain which.

As Fr. Hill down-shifted gears from all-out sprint to somewhere between second and first gear, I glimpsed the object of his concern. An ancient and tottering scarecrow of a man was attempting to jaywalk across busy Jackson Street unassisted.

The priest and I negotiated our way across the street in time to catch the man before he tumbled headlong into the street to be crushed beneath a torrent of on-coming traffic. I caught the man by his torso, thinking I was holding fast to a living skeleton. I could feel absolutely no meat on this old man's bones.

Only his occasional groans spoke of life.

This man's tattered shirt had been reduced to a rag, and yet it still contained sufficient buttons to be about one-third of the way wrapped around what had once been a belly. A pocket of sorts had formed where the shirt was tucked into a pair of dingy trousers. And inside that ersatz pocket I discovered what appeared to be at least a million bugs, all of which were now stampeding their way to some kind of freedom.

Right away I recognized the bugs as a telltale sign of this man's recent circumstances. He had spent some time in a dumpster.

With slow and gentle steps, Fr. Hill and I led him into the soup kitchen. I then directed him to the shower room while my colleague searched in our small clothing room for some suitable clothes to cover this old man, once I'd gotten him cleaned up and bug free.

Within seconds, I found myself in a shower stall with the naked skeleton of a man who could not have been a day younger than ninety. As I attempted to hand him a clean washrag and a new bar of soap, he turned away from me, tears streaming down his face. This move convinced me of what I previously suspected—this old man was lost in the haze of dementia.

I soaped up the washrag and went right to work scrubbing his skin and bones all the while doing my best to remain as dry as possible. I smiled as I whispered to myself, "So, this is why I went to seminary and bothered to learn Hebrew and Greek."

Within minutes we were finished and the old man was clean while the shower's floor was filled with at least a shovel full of dead and dying bugs.

The next moment, Fr. Hill appeared at the shower room's door to present the old man with a suit of clothes replete with boxers and a shirt that probably had never enjoyed any commerce whatsoever with an iron. A few minutes later, we had him dressed in a suit that didn't actually fit.

The pant cuffs hit him about a foot above his ankles, but we decided we could rectify this fashion disaster with a pair of long dark socks. The waist was four times too big, but we corrected this problem with a donated plastic belt that gathered in enough material to make a whole other pair of pants. We more-than-less tied a pair of dress shoes to his feet before we requested him to stand so that we might admire our handiwork and his makeover.

He looked, at least, unsoiled and comfortable, which, after all, had been our goal. He was not ready for the red carpet, or even church for that matter, but we had gotten him scrubbed and then dressed him in the best we had on hand. For us, this was enough, simply because this was the very best we could do for him.

I led him to my office where I invited him to sit for a spell. He declined my offer of a cup of coffee with a smile that revealed all of his teeth were missing. His face was worn, beaten, and appeared permanently pointed in the unmistakable direction of despair.

I did my best to hold a smile that he might find reassuring. At last, I deigned to say, "What is your name?"

His toothless smile signaled nothing more than the acknowledgement of my question.

Trying again, I extended my had to him and said, "My name is Bob. What's your name?"

Again, no answer. He took my hand and once more only offered his ridiculous toothless grin.

Frustrated, I wondered what to do with him. If I drove him

to our shelter, he would very likely wander away and be forever lost. I could neither take him home nor allow him to sleep in my office. I considered calling the police, but I suspected they would not take him.

Next, he offered me a slip of paper no bigger than a gum wrapper. Somehow the thing had survived the shower. Surprised, but now strangely exhilarated, I took it and unfolded it to discover a seven-digit phone number plus an area code I recognized to be New York City.

The old man stared at the floor, thus signaling he was done with questions to which he held no answers. I dialed the number. A man's voice answered.

Once I introduced myself and explained the reason for my call, the man on the other end yelled, "Helen, someone has found Albert and he's alive in Dallas."

"Oh, thank God!" the woman hollered back from a distance.

The man spoke to me again. "Tell me again where you are and how much you want to send him home."

"I will drive him to DFW and put him on a plane to New York. I will call you with further details once I know them."

If the man on the other end said 'thank you,' I failed to hear it.

In a flash, I called an airline and only by God's grace managed to reserve a seat on nonstop flight to New York City that would depart in about three hours. I strapped Albert into the front seat of my small Toyota and headed to the airport where I parked illegally against a curb in order to dash inside and secure his ticket.

By the time I returned to my car, three parking tickets flapped under the wiper blade, each one from a different authority. Albert remained securely bound in the seat belt and, thank God, had not wandered away. At a very slow pace, I managed to ease him into the terminal where I placed him in a seat close to the ticket counter. Realizing that I had to move my car before it got towed, I begged a lovely young woman, dressed in the airline's uniform, to sit with Albert until I returned. To my astonishment, she agreed.

By the time I returned, she had managed to strike up a genuine conversation with the same old man who had found it a major ordeal even to utter syllables to me. I chuckled as her eyes met mine.

"You all seem to be getting along well," I said.

"Oh, we're old friends now." She returned to her counter and Albert sniffled until he cried.

"What's wrong, Albert?"

No answer. He stared at the floor once more and shook like a frightened pup.

I next said, "Albert, have you ever flown before?"

He wagged his head in the direction of 'no.'

"Are you afraid to fly?"

He nodded an emphatic 'yes!'

"Albert the most dangerous part of this trip was our drive out here in Dallas traffic. Flying is the easy part."

Albert's silent stare said it all, proving my words both unnecessary and wholly ineffective. I eased out of the chair and once more approached the woman behind the counter. She agreed to give Albert priority boarding and even to have a flight attendant locate two unreserved and adjacent seats where she could sit with him during takeoff and hold his hand.

When the flight was ready for boarding, I walked Albert to the concourse where a pretty young attendant met us. She called him by name as she took his hand. Albert's vacant smile spoke volumes about something, although I'm not certain exactly what.

Right away, I headed to a pay telephone where I placed a call to New York. This time the man who answered spoke with the warmth of newfound gratitude in his voice.

I provided him with the details. He promised to meet Albert at the airport and take him home where he and Albert's sister would take good care of him and never let him wander away again.

Exhausted from the strain of it all, I dropped into a chair facing a huge window. And as I watched the big jet with Albert on board take off and head north into the darkness, I realized that for the last several hours I had unwittingly become a part of a microcosmic drama illustrating well the human condition:

For like old Albert, all of us get lost from time to time, and in our lost state we are vulnerable to the toxic contaminants of this world as we find ourselves naked, alone, afraid, and desperate. In such dark hours, all we know to do is to search for any light that might show us the way home. That light we finally discover is God's love, which is forever our guide out of the darkness, or as an ancient psalmist so powerfully and so succinctly put it:

"The Lord is my light and my salvation." (Psalm 27:1)

CHAPTER 4

The Way

So how did old Albert locate the soup kitchen? Many times over the years, I've been asked that question. The only reasonable answer I can give is that even in the unforgiving fog of dementia he was somehow mysteriously led.

Furthermore, I am now convinced that his decision to seek help in our soup kitchen was not his alone, but rather a collaborative effort on the part of what little remained of his still conscious mind and the Holy Spirit. Paul tells us that the Spirit prays for us, and I believe this occurs when we can no longer pray for ourselves.

This should not surprise us because every journey out of the false self and into a whole new life in the true self always begins with prayer. Either we ask God to deliver us from the self we made up out of perceived necessity or we must rely upon the Holy Spirit to make the request for us. Whichever path we take, we must always be guided and supported by earnest prayer if we hope to find our way into the light where the true self abides.

Long ago I arrived at a regional conference center where I was scheduled to lead a weekend retreat. As I registered at the front desk, I encountered the center's director. The man concerned me a bit by appearing anxious to the point of trembling. All I knew about him was that, in his brief tenure as director, he had earned a reputation for being a bit callous to not only to his staff, but also to the center's guests as well. On the afternoon of my arrival I learned that he was required to meet with the center's board that very evening to show why he should not be terminated.

He greeted me at the front door and requested a few minutes of my time, which I was glad to offer him as together we stepped away from the registration desk and into a conversation area with several comfortable chairs. Once seated, we both waited for the other to speak.

At last, I broke the silence by asking him what was on his mind. He seemed to be masking an ocean of fear with a thin veneer of what I suspected was habituated anger.

As he wove a tale of being highly effective, but terribly misunderstood, I found myself wishing I were some place else, doing most anything else. I really didn't want to listen because this man was not willing to do much more than blame others for his situation. Nevertheless, his fear of being humiliated later that day struck a chord of compassion in my soul, so I decided to pay attention as he accused others for causing his current tenuous situation.

The longer he kept up the blame game, the more his words sounded to me like a clanging gong that hurt my ears. As I sat with him and nodded, I wondered what he thought he might accomplish by filling the air with rage and accusations.

I once genuinely liked this man and I'd always enjoyed a distant, but pleasant enough, relationship with him. But on this day, if I realized anything at all, it was that he was so mired in his rage and attendant self-righteousness that nothing I could say or do would really be of help to him in any way.

Perhaps a certain amount of catharsis is good for the mind as well as for the soul, but this was not catharsis so much as the ranting of a narcissistic perfectionist whose fragile ego had been wounded by his staff's rebellion against his abusive management style. What this man could not even begin to comprehend was that his failure was not in his performance as a director, but rather in his refusal to love the very people he had been charged to direct. In his mind, he'd done most everything well. He'd kept the place in the black and had successfully marketed the center, thus significantly increasing the annual income.

However, he'd accomplished these two goals at enormous emotional expense to his employees and to himself. And now sitting before me was an uproariously successful executive trembling at the idea of enduring the humiliation of being terminated.

Once he paused to breathe, I asked him if he really believed he might be fired. When he answered in the affirmative, I gave consideration to congratulating him, but thought better of the idea because he would hear my words as somewhere between sarcastic and cruel. I wisely remained silent except to excuse myself to join the group I'd come to lead in a retreat.

Why would I consider congratulating a man in such obvious pain? For me the answer was as simple as it was obvious:

This man had hit his own kind of bottom, and bottom is the place in our lives where God can do his best healing work if, that is, we will only allow that healing work to be done. For it's only at the bottom where we see and finally get it that our way of doing life does not work.

Even more, we grow in understanding that our way of doing this life has caused us to fall on our face and to experience the excruciating sting of rejection. Jesus described this agonizing condition as a distinct blessing in these words:

> "Blessed are the poor in spirit, for theirs is the kingdom of heaven."
>
> (Matthew 5:3)

At first reading these words appear counterintuitive and confusing. Nevertheless, with some careful thought given to them, we begin to see that it is our self-inflicted pain and suffering that compels and drives us to discover a whole new way to be a human being, and this new way Jesus described as "the kingdom of heaven."

The false self cannot even begin to enter this kingdom because its bloated ego cannot possibly squeeze through the kingdom's narrow gates. Jesus once told of this impossible squeeze by describing the phenomenon as the absurdity of a huge camel attempting to squeeze through the tiny eye of a needle. (Mark 10:25)

As hard as we might try, it cannot possibly be done.

Only one solution gains us entrance to the kingdom, and that is, the false self must first die, and take with it the well-defended ego. And this is the most daunting challenge any human being can be asked—actually, commanded—to accept and then accomplish.

At first this challenge feels like a real impossibility because we have invested an entire lifetime carefully constructing, protecting, and promoting this homemade self. We not only value this self, but we also cherish it because we have more or less effectively defended it for the whole of our lives.

And let's face it. The self we've cobbled together is really all we know. As a consequence, we must pray for guidance and divine assistance in order to accomplish what we cannot do on our own.

So how does this process of dying to the old self work?

The only reasonable answer is to say that every such death is both unique and invariably mysterious, but Jesus put it this way:

> "For those who want to save their life will lose it, and those who lose their life for my sake, and for the sake of the gospel, will save it."
>
> (Matthew 16:25)

And while he proclaimed this paradox of dying to the old self, he never offered a simple step-by-step process or told us either where or how to begin. In my own unique experience, I discovered prayer as the beginning point, and my friends in Alcoholics Anonymous have assisted me greatly in this discovery.

In the past 25 years, I've come to see recovering alcoholics and addicts as the real experts in what it means to discover and to live one day at a time in the true self. Typically, although not always, I have come to trust recovering people to live in the truth because they have been to hell and know with certainty they don't want to go back.

The fact is I trust their kind of transformation far more than I do that of most evangelical Christians who with such pride proclaim to be born again. Far too often, evangelical Christians view their personal rebirth as a spiritual merit badge that distinguishes them from us "lesser folk."

Every expression of pride is out of alignment with God's will. Therefore, the true self is never prideful. The recovering person can be counted on to be humble, since he or she would much prefer to confess past sins than boast of recovery from the disease of addiction. Furthermore, these folks will be far more interested in speaking of God's grace than they will be of portraying themselves as something special.

To put it in succinct terms, I've encountered many born again Christians in the past 40 years who would do very well to be born again-again. Perhaps this is why I found it far more comfortable to work in a soup kitchen with street drunks and the profoundly mentally ill, and also in a recovery center with addicts and alcoholics, than I ever did in the church.

Recovering people have convinced me that the key to their recovery has always been the practice of simplicity. In other words, they have a way of keeping everything in their lives simple and honest with their primary and passionate goal being to remain clean, straight, sober, and dedicated to the truth in every facet of their lives.

During my tenure as chaplain in a recovery center, I came to know and to befriend many men and women who were dedicated to working the 12 steps of recovery. Almost to a person, they told me their healing began with the simple one-word prayer, "Help!"

I recall one client in particular at the recovery center who, after one of my classes, informed me he was determined to bolt and return to street life where he could use again and get high every time he felt the need. Of course, I encouraged the man to stay in treatment and to trust both God and the program.

When I returned days later to teach another class, I was delighted to discover this man grinning at me from his place on the front row.

Years later, I happened into him again as I entered a local

pancake house where he waited tables while wearing clean clothes and a bright blue apron. His hair was now short and combed and his face clean-shaven.

He could tell right off I did not recognize him because he set the coffee pot on the table and offered his hand as he reintroduced himself to me. Right away, he reported that he had been clean, straight, and sober for a bit more than two years and was attending at least three AA meetings a week.

After congratulating him on his new life, I asked what kept him in recovery when he had once been so desperate to return to his old life on the streets.

He offered a one-word answer. "Prayer." Then he smiled. "Only prayer."

Sliding into the booth opposite me uninvited, he explained: "I was literally heading out the door when I remembered that you folks were attempting to teach us that 'God is love.' (1st John 4:8) And that's when it hit me that I wasn't going to find any love on the streets, so I turned around and went back through the door. And I've been on the right path ever since."

Jesus tells us that we will mourn, and we do, indeed, experience mourning when we dare to die to the false self. Mourning is a form of suffering, and suffering, of course, means pain. Who wants to bring on any kind of self-inflicted pain when we can avoid it? The slam-dunk reality of real mourning is what prevents most people from dying to the false self and its myriad complex ego defenses.

It's much easier to remain in the false self and to continue living mired in its painful habit of generating and expressing self-interested thoughts and emotions—or living forever 'poor in spirit'—than it is to die to this self. The choice lies always with us: we can live and enjoy a peaceful existence grounded in love or we can merely exist living a life driven primarily by fear.

Psychotherapy done correctly is always a discovery process. In other words, the psychotherapist who knows what he or she is doing always works to empower the client to discover his or her own unique truth. And this is so because it is not the truth until the client can first discover it, and then embrace it, and at last own it.

For the most part, I was successful in empowering folks to discover their own unique truths. However, there was one client with whom I failed miserably. I did my best to help him discover that his emotional abuse of his wife was most likely linked inextricably to his mother's emotional abuse of him as a child.

As hard as I tried, I could not make him see any possible connection. In the long run, I concluded he could discern no connection because he had learned in childhood to protect and defend his mother at all costs.

As a result, I found myself stuck in a bizarre impasse with this man. He refused to recognize what could have been an important clue to the mystery of his long-standing anger with and subsequent abuse of his wife. And he refused to see it, because to do so would be to attack his mother, a woman he had long imagined he was obliged to defend, and yet, he'd been alienated from her for more than two decades. In the meantime, he abused his wife as a way of venting the unconscious anger he had felt toward his mother.

The harder I worked to help him discover this connection, the more he resisted and the more he turned up the volume on abusing his wife. It was as though this man lived for anger.

In fact, in him I could find no other emotion. Either this man was aware of being angry, or he was asleep. If any love remained in his heart, it had been eclipsed by the dark shadows of rage. And there was a sense in which his anger did work for him, because, in his own mind, at least, anger kept him from being all-out depressed while it drove him to greater and greater success and more and more money.

One icy winter morning, I at last realized he was just paying me to spar with him in front of his very frustrated wife once a week in the narcissistic cause of proving to her—and even more, to me—that, without question, he was the smartest person in the room.

Having reached all-out frustration with him and wanting our relationship to end, I said, "So how do you think you're doing in this marriage?"

"Great!" He offered this one-word answer with a knowing grin.

With that, his wife jumped to her feet and screamed, "That's it! I'm done!" She stormed out of my office.

For the first time in our weeks of work together, he scrambled to his feet and wailed, "What do I do now?"

In as caring a tone as I could manage I said, " John, (not his real name) you would benefit from a major spiritual awakening. And the only way you are going to accomplish that is to join a recovery group and work the 12 Steps."

"But I'm not an alcoholic!"

"I know that, but like alcoholics and addicts, you stand in dire need of a wake-up call. The end product of all successful 12 Step work is not only sobriety, but even more, it is a authentic spiritual awakening."

"I don't understand."

"That's because you've never worked a program."

I then rose to my feet to stand face-to-face and nose-to-nose with this bully. "Look, John, talk therapy alone will very likely not produce the results you want. You're going to have to do some heavy lifting, if you want to keep your marriage."

He both pondered and questioned the invitation for the remainder of our hour together, and then departed my office with a handshake and the first words of gratitude I'd ever heard him speak. I have no idea if he ever joined a 12 Step group, because I never heard from him following our handshake.

So why did I make this suggestion? The answer is simple: because I have come to believe that spiritual awakening is not the province of psychology, or even counseling, but rather the goal of all good spirituality. We worship God and study scripture so that we might be awakened to our true purpose in this life, which is to balance our lives on the three-legged stool, or in other words, to love God, our neighbors and ourselves. Psychology alone cannot accomplish this, but the 12 Steps of recovery can and does every day.

And why is this so? The answer lies in the origin of the 12 Steps.

Did these 12 steps fall out of heaven? No.

Should they be included in the canon as holy writ? Again, the answer is no.

They did not fall out of heaven, but they are in part extrapolated from the Beatitudes, which are pure Jesus in that they are so counterintuitive, so mysterious and, most of all, so incredibly healing.

A former colleague, the late Rev. Dr. Gerald Mann, was fond of describing these steps as "The Gospel in drag." While Dr. Mann was well known for being a bit salty at times, I agree that these steps place our feet on the same spiritual path, as do the four Gospels.

For example, like with the 12 Steps, the Beatitudes begin at the bottom, where we find ourselves poor in spirit. Upon the discovery of our condition, we realize only that we want out of this place. And this is where we encounter bad news and good news at the same time.

The bad news is that we must die to the false self and the good news is that we will be comforted as we do. If we dare to die to the egocentric self we created, we will discover that we will experience pain. Without doubt we will mourn.

But again, this discovery is followed by the very good news that we will be comforted. The Holy Spirit will not permit us to languish and twist in the wind. In ways we cannot imagine, God will show up to comfort us as the Spirit delivers us from the pain of mourning the death of the ever-voracious ego.

As we awaken from our period of mourning where our pain and confusion have brought us closer than ever to God, we discover much to our surprise that we are becoming meek. And we find ourselves questioning the nature and the very essence of all that it means to be meek.

This is not at all easy because in this world meekness is such a rare commodity. When I was a kid growing up, not one time did I hear anyone—not my parents, not my teachers, not my coaches, not my friends, not even a preacher—encourage me to be meek.

However, I did often receive such messages as:

"Be strong."
"Be tough."
"Don't cry."
"Be confident."
"Don't fail."
"Don't embarrass the family."
"Be a winner."

"Always do your best."

As a result, I had difficulty knowing what it meant to be meek. In the world that raised me, meekness was synonymous with weakness. Or to be meek meant to be a coward. And to be viewed as a coward in my youth was equivalent to declaring yourself a social outcast. Most of us really didn't engage in fights, but we did our best to exude a 'don't mess with me' image. In Texas, this thing is known as swagger and when you're a teenage boy, you'd better have it or you are a bit suspect, at best.

One of my former psychotherapist colleagues once told me a story of a boy from West Texas who came close to getting himself seriously injured and even permanently impaired by trying out for his high school football team. This kid had absolutely no athletic talent and only weighed a bit more than 100 pounds; nevertheless, he did his best to impress the coaches of a perennial high school football power because he was terrified of being viewed by his peers as gay.

Needless to say, he never made the team and later enrolled in the University of Texas at which time he sought the services of my colleague in order to work on his self-esteem and body image issues. But like most adolescent males in Texas, he equated being meek with being effeminate or gay. With the help of my former colleague, this young man finally did accept himself and graduated from the university to become a highly respected and beloved public school teacher in his community.

So exactly what is meekness? For starters, it is harnessed power. The meek are strong people with strong personalities who have learned that all real strength lies in the ability to respond appropriately rather than to react emotionally. Only the true self can be meek because the false self perceives every affront to the precious ego as a cause célèbre and as a justification for retaliation or worse violence. Only the truly meek can turn the other cheek; hence only the meek can and do regularly rise above retribution.

I once knew such a man who was a beloved assistant football coach in our high school. Physically, he was a grizzly bear of a man who had won three letters in football at a major university prior to coming to Dallas to teach and to coach. I knew him even before I entered high school because he and his fine family were members of the same church where my family and I attended. Throughout the whole of my life, I viewed him as wise, gentle, and most of all kind. As far as I know, the adults in our church regarded him as a good man with a gentle spirit and a kind heart, and as a superb role model for kids.

Throughout my high school career, this coach would regularly pull me aside to check with me regarding my wellbeing. On the practice field he was a no-nonsense disciplinarian who demanded 110% from his players, but in the classroom and in the hallways, he was a gentleman in the truest sense of the word. He was always polite, gracious, and mannerly, especially in the presence of women. He never used foul language and could always be counted on to offer wisdom to every situation.

To many of his players he was the solid father figure they did not have at home. To me, he was a man to be both respected and greatly admired.

Every day during lunch in my senior year, I sat at a table in the school cafeteria we designated from day 1 as 'the senior table.' No junior or sophomore boy could possibly be allowed admission to our sacred 'senior table.' For the most part, we were unremarkable boys who looked forward to graduation in a few months so that we might begin in earnest figuring out how to avoid becoming just so much cannon fodder in Vietnam.

Central to our way of coping with the existential anxiety that attends the prospect of an early death was to plot mischief. One ridiculous game we played was to dare each other to do something really stupid, such as drop a live roach in the cafeteria's mash potatoes or approach a senior girl and tell her every one of us thought she was beautiful, or deliberately drop a full water glass so it shattered on the concrete floor thus causing the entire lunchroom of several hundred to erupt in applause and squeals of delight. For us, to take a dare and to act on it was a visible illustration of our manly courage.

Our nonsense was in the main harmless until the day my friend Mitch, a guy who'd probably played too much football without a helmet, dared James to hurl an apple at our beloved coach and hit him squarely in the head. I chuckled because I knew James would never be so reckless as to throw an apple at a man who could have broken him into pieces like he was nothing more than so many pieces of kindling.

I gasped in abject incredulity as James jumped to his feet and reached back to hurl the apple at the coach like it was a fastball splitting home plate right down dead center. With no time for me to catch my breath, the apple exploded on the back of the coach's head like it was a grenade. Apple pulp and red skin flew everywhere. An uneasy hush filled that lunchroom like a biblical plague bringing to the room certain death.

I couldn't bear to witness the coming wrath, so I bowed my head and squeezed my eyes shut and prayed to God I'd never have to open them again. At last I did force them open them to glimpse through a veil of tears the giant of a man strolling toward me all the while wiping apple pulp from his forehead and neck with a handkerchief.

When he arrived at my place at the table, he rested his hand upon my shoulder in a way that summoned me to look up at his familiar face. As I looked him squarely in the eye, he said, "Bobby, I've known you all of your life. Isn't that right?"

"Yes sir," I squeaked.

"I know you and your character, and I know you didn't throw that apple."

"No sir, I did not."

"But you know who threw it, don't you?"

"Yes sir, I do." I said, now trembling.

"And if I ask you to tell me who threw it, you would."

"Yes sir, I would."

"But if you told me who threw it, you'd lose face with your friends here at this table. Isn't that right?"

"Yes sir."

"Well then, I'm not going to do that to you. So, I guess I'll just never know who threw that apple." And with that he walked away still casually wiping his head with the handkerchief.

And on that unforgettable afternoon, I witnessed a powerful example of true meekness. As I have reflected upon that incident for the past half-century plus a few years, I've come to the conclusion that on that day in the dingy and drab high school lunchroom, I witnessed in its most powerful expression one of Jesus' beatitudes.

* * *

And Jesus tells us that the meek shall inherit the Earth. So what does this mean?

The answer is simple because it is contained in my memory of the football coach walking quietly and peacefully away from his assailant all the while demonstrating to us and to everyone in that lunchroom that meekness is the only real and lasting expression of strength.

And because this man had somehow grown far beyond the need to retaliate, everyone who witnessed his meekness glimpsed the future Jesus prophesied when he prayed the words, "Thy Kingdom come."

Of course, we had no idea what we witnessed, even though most of us were at least somewhat familiar with the Beatitudes. Nevertheless, in that moment we witnessed the intersection of the future tense with the present tense.

Jesus taught us to pray for that day to come when most people would be so truly meek as to give up the reflexive need to retaliate in any way. The meek will, indeed, inherit the Earth the day Jesus' immortal prayer is fulfilled and the kingdom finally does arrive.

And on that day, all wars will cease and all people everywhere will come to view their former enemies as brothers and sisters. And on that day, mercy will replace retribution and love will be declared the victor at long last.

Meekness acquires new appetites. Whereas the voracious ego hungers for all that which will enhance its image in the world's skewed view, the meek hunger for righteousness.

Long ago I visited with a most remarkable man who had dedicated his entire being to building a working ranch east of Austin so that his Down's Syndrome daughter and others like her might have a safe place to live and to work for years. As we walked together across empty pastureland waiting to be fenced and filled with hungry animals, I asked him how he planned to bring to fruition what appeared to me to be an audacious, if not impossible, dream.

His answer was so succinct and poignant as to write itself

upon my heart: He said, "Oh, I just plan to do the next right thing until this ranch is up and running and about 50 or so young people can enjoy a quality lifestyle every day of their lives."

Today his ranch is 'up and running' and has even been featured in the national press. As far as I am concerned, his ranch is the product of disciplined righteousness.

This man is deeply satisfied, probably far beyond what most of us ever know in our lifetimes, because most of us allow our insatiable egos to drive our lives and our shallow faith. Status, money, and influence may taste as good as some five-star restaurant's exquisite dessert, but these things never satisfy our deep soulful hunger. As Jesus tells us, righteousness is all that can fill us to the point of satisfaction. But we don't and can't know this until we first become genuinely meek.

This beatitude regarding righteousness segues perfectly into the next since mercy is the natural expression of the meek and mercy can be counted on to be always right. The meek express mercy because mercy is their core identity. Mercy is not something they do so much as it is who they are.

One spiritual axiom I posit to be incontrovertible is that all meek souls have been touched by grace in a powerful way. Thus, all meek souls know what it means to experience forgiveness, and because they do, they give grace freely and, in time, even reflexively. The meek know a secret that is lost on most people

And that secret is this paradox: They must give grace away if they hope to keep it.

In my four-plus decades of experience as a pastor, I've yet to meet a resentful human being who was happy, much less at peace. If we are ever to know any real lasting peace in our lives, we must first learn to practice the challenging art of forgiveness.

And we best learn that art by first asking people to forgive us.

My hunch is that once we become meek enough to ask for and then to receive forgiveness, we will learn for ourselves how to give it to others. And in asking others to forgive us, we assist them in keeping the grace they themselves have received. So then, as strange as it sounds, every request for forgiveness is truly a benevolent act. In other words, we do a person a favor in asking them to forgive us.

If I were to be invited to serve as the pastor of a church again (which is impossible at my age), I would accept the call only if the congregation agreed to make the practice of forgiveness central to its adult education program. I would assist in writing a curriculum that offered opportunities to keep a weekly journal of their own individual forgiveness experiences throughout each week, and for the first year of my tenure in that church I would preach forgiveness until I was hoarse from the effort. I would write about forgiveness in every church communication, and I would lead four all-church retreats on the topic of forgiveness in that first year alone.

And in doing this, I would pray that the people I serve might learn something about the character of God and about what it means to live life as a meek, mercy-giving human being. And if the idea and practice of forgiveness were to metastasize and take hold in other churches, a spiritual movement of radical forgiveness could give rise to a new spiritual revolution that would have a dramatic impact our strife-ridden culture.

Meek people would become the majority and grace would become the cultural norm. And for the very first time in human history, more people than not would claim to be happy, and some might even say the age in which they live is finally "on Earth is as it is in heaven."

Of course, this is nothing more than one old used-up preacher's pipe dream; nevertheless, I am convinced that if people were finally willing to be merciful first and everything else later on, our world would be radically and forever changed. And I believe this to be true because I know Jesus believed it to be true.

CHAPTER 5

Peacemaking

The apex of our spiritual journey is reached when at last we become genuine peacemakers. All along, the perceived end of our journey has been to draw closer and closer to God. And once we have become capable of making peace, the Son of God tells us that our blessing will be to be called the children of God.

But the question remains: but who will call us that?

We know the world will probably not call us the children of God because the next two beatitudes warn us that we will very likely be persecuted. So who will know us as "the children of God?"

The only answer can be Christ Himself. This is so because, as we enter into the difficult and even sometimes dangerous business of peacemaking in our war-torn culture, we will become the brothers and sisters of Jesus Christ and, therefore, "the children of God."

Why is peacemaking so difficult, and why does it invite such a reflexive punitive reaction from the world?

The answer to the first question is rather obvious: peace is not the norm in this world. Conflict is! When someone says, "I want peace," what he or she is up to, unbeknownst to themselves, is to make the concept of peace a goal of the ego.

The word "want" connotes desire. And where the ego desires anything at all, there is always yearning and longing, and hence, no peace. If led by the ego alone, we will begin every quest for peace with an innate, deep-seated conflict stewing about within our souls. And because we can only realize peace by first becoming peaceful within ourselves, making peace is difficult at best, and impossible for most people since most of us have no clue as to how even to begin the process.

The effective peacemakers in this world are those few who have grown so mature spiritually that their very lives provide the world with a glimpse, and nothing more than that, of Jesus' proclamation of the 'Kingdom of God.'

Every human endeavor bent on solving a problem, no matter how noble or sacred, can be counted on to begin with conflict, because every human endeavor involves the ego. When it comes to making peace, we don't check our egos at the door when we enter our workplaces, our homes or, even our churches.

No, what we invariably do is convince ourselves that we know the solution to whatever conflict we face, if only we can persuade, or worse, force others to join us in the challenge of bringing to full fruition our strategy. This coercive approach never works, at least not in the long term, because in the end coercion gives rise to resentment the way stagnant rain puddles produce mosquitoes in summer. The best coercion can do is to install a temporary status quo that merely mimics peace.

The second question is: why does the world persecute those who earnestly and passionately attempt to make peace?

The world persecutes peacemakers because peacemaking is invariably an expression of love. Those who love with such depth and courage as to live as Christ lived—and thereby dare to become his brother or sister—seriously threaten the world in which we live.

Jesus came, not to bring a new religion into this world, but rather to proclaim a whole new reality he alternately called "the Kingdom of God" and "the Kingdom of Heaven." Under either name, it is the same thing: a new kingdom where love is the foundation, where justice is the organizing principle, and where peace is the norm.

Jesus' proclamation of this kingdom was, as much as anything else, what got him killed by ancient Rome. Even today, people are threatened by any talk that threatens the status quo, and this is why Dr. Martin Luther King, Jr., was slain. His kind of love pointed to the very kingdom Jesus proclaimed, and thereby, threatened long-established traditions, mores, and folkways that for centuries had been perceived by the majority to be sacred. Dr. King was the American prophet of non-violence, and yet he met with a violent end because he threatened to bring in a whole new social order predicated upon love.

When I was in college, I was privileged to take a course entitled 'The History of World War II.' Following an arduous semester of lectures, readings, and papers, I sat for the final exam which was to be a three-hour ordeal where I would be called upon to write feverishly, and even frenetically, to earn the letter grade of "A." This exam consisted of only one question, which was as simple as it proved daunting.

The question was this: "World War II. Why?"

After reading it, I walked to the professor's desk where I picked up four blank exam books before returning to my desk to write a response. I began by outlining the punitive indignities imposed upon Germany by the Treaty of Versailles and then traced the influence of "the Great Depression" upon the

German economy.

I was but a few minutes into composing my comprehensive, if still somewhat desperate, essay when a fellow classmate and friend turned in his completed test booklet. This young man was a stellar student, regarded by the faculty and his peers alike as extraordinarily talented. His sudden departure so disturbed me I read the test question again.

I could only wonder if this were some kind of trick question requiring only a very simple and quick answer. Of course, the test question had not changed since my first reading, so I gave up the idea and decided not to worry about my friend's early departure.

Days later I happened into him, and I inquired about his grade on the exam. As nonchalantly as if he were giving me tomorrow's weather forecast, he said, "Oh, I made an 'F'."

Shifting my weight from one foot to the other as though attempting to run away lest I be infected with failure, I demanded to know what he'd written in his exam book.

He smiled and said, "Oh, I read the question as to the why of World War II, and I wrote, 'Because this world finds it easier to hate than to love.' And because old Dr. Doe_____ doesn't have a sense of humor, I bombed the course, but that's okay because I was admitted to graduate school last semester."

"But why did you write what you wrote?

"Because it is the truth!"

For half a century since, I've pondered both the veracity and the courage contained in that brilliant young man's answer. Although I made an "A" on that final exam and the same grade in the course, I've long thought that my friend's parsimonious response was terribly profound and in no way flippant, dismissive, or disrespectful. Rather, I've always regarded his answer as far, far superior to my four-bluebook diatribe.

My friend's answer was the truth; while my essay consisted of nothing more than the regurgitation of the details I had gleaned from the course lectures and readings.

Several years ago, I was invited to preach at a newly formed church that met in an old warehouse. As I entered the warehouse, I spied a hand-lettered sign that read: "If you begin with hate, you've already lost!"

This sentiment is an appropriate hermeneutic for any congregation. I read into it an implicit invitation to join with these people in beginning the life-long journey out of the false self and into the self created by God for the holy purpose of establishing His Kingdom right here and right now on Earth.

The autumn I entered seminary, the war in Vietnam had reached a political tipping point. It was obvious, even to the likes of Walter Cronkite, South Vietnam was soon to fall to the communists. Richard Nixon was so determined not to be the first American president to lose a war that he escalated the conflict by bombing North Vietnamese cities indiscriminately and by sending even more troops into Southeast Asia.

The students at the University of Texas decided that enough was enough. They organized a student-led moratorium that was to consist of a classroom 'walk out' followed by a giant peace march.

Out of deference to the seminary's donor base, most of whom were both wealthy and politically conservative Presbyterians, the seminary president met us halfway. He refused to cancel classes but he did inform us that we would be in no way punished for missing class and that we were free to spend the day as we saw fit.

Filled with angst that morning regarding everything from

my personal future to this terrible war, I made my way to the seminary chapel. Most of my fellow students and the majority of the faculty filled the pews.

A heavy pall hung over the small sanctuary like a cloud waiting to decide in favor of erupting or remaining benign. I joined a new friend on the back row and bowed my head in the futile attempt to pray. However, I could in no way believe in the efficacy of prayer in that dark moment. Things were too big, events too violent, dynamics too out of control, and my own heart far too dark for me to dare utter what I knew would be nothing more than one of my silly sophomoric petitions.

Thus, I only pretended to pray as I waited for someone to fill the empty pulpit and provide some kind of leadership. At last, our homiletics professor, a rotund little man who loved his students with legendary pastoral concern, climbed into the pulpit. He announced that packing boxes covered in butcher paper were being set up in the chapel's small narthex for our use as what he called "proclamation sites."

We were then invited to file in decent Presbyterian order to the rear of the chapel and write a proclamation. I jumped to my feet and joined the line. When I arrived at a box, I simply wrote the truth: "I cannot pray!"

Feeling at the same time ridiculous and relieved, I inched my way to the door and made the one-block walk to the South Mall on the University of Texas campus. Thousands of angry students were gathered and responding wildly to the anti-war rants of student leaders armed with powerful bullhorns.

The morning was unseasonably warm, even for early October, so I found a shade tree separated by several yards from the so-called 'peace rally,' and I reclined there to observe and to listen while I questioned myself as to why I could not pray. I first imagined I was too filled with anxiety to offer any authentic petition to God, but then I admitted to myself that anxiety was not the cause.

Sitting on the periphery of a mass of raging students was not my idea of the solitude required to provide an environment conducive to prayer. As I rose from my place in the live oak tree's benevolent shade, the crowd's passion hit a crescendo and with it an uninvited truth invaded my mind and refused to be exorcised by my usual rationalizations or other tricks.

And as clearly as if a friend spoke directly to me, a voice in my own head said, "You can't pray because your heart is full of hatred."

As best I know to describe it, the voice I heard was what I've learned in the years since to call "the voice of truth." In that difficult moment in my youth, I had to admit to myself that, like it or not, I was indeed filled with hatred.

I hated President Richard Nixon and his administration for escalating a war that never should have been waged. I hated every American who supported the war. I hated the ubiquitous bumper stickers that read, " Love it or leave it." I hated the draft that had compelled my boyhood friends to die for a cause that in reality was another nation's civil war. I hated the war, but most of all I hated myself for being so weak and indecisive in an age that required both courage and enormous conviction.

My parents were opposed to the war, but they were also strangely opposed to me being opposed it. People of courage and conviction had marched for civil rights only a few years before, and now I saw it as my time to stand up and be counted as a bona fide "war protestor," both in my family and in my home church back in Dallas.

I remained in the tree's shade for a while longer while I

searched for mentors. I was still young enough and inexperienced enough to need a role model in the form of someone I both respected and trusted to show me the right path to follow.

As I wondered what the faculty back at the seminary was up to, I spied a young professor joining the slow-moving march. His participation emboldened me to wonder how Dr. Stuart Currie was spending his morning on this moratorium day.

This man was by far the most respected professor on campus. As students, we not only respected him, we revered him. We regarded his intellect as immeasurable and his faith as deep and as solid as that of an ancient prophet right out of the Old Testament. He was a true genius with the heart of a saint. And while he didn't suffer fools gladly, he could be counted on to be ever compassionate and always kind even to students, who like me, were quite limited intellectually.

I remained under the tree, hoping I might spot him and follow his lead, because I knew that whatever he was doing was right and always of God. But I failed to spot him, and the mass of students was now moving and fast heading south on its way to what was then the South Congress Bridge.

At long last, I lifted myself from the ground and joined the march. As we abandoned the University's South Mall, we flowed into Austin's Guadalupe Street where we were met by a sidewalk lined with people who opposed our protest. Some of the bystanders hurled insults at us or tossed paper cups filled with hot coffee into our midst as we slowly passed by. I'd never experienced anything like this in my life. Before we could travel a block south, we were threatened, abused verbally, and even spat upon by our fellow-citizens, many of whom I suspected were church-going Christians.

And that's when it dawned on me that I had been drawn to

this rally and subsequent march because it had been billed as a 'peace march.' But this was certainly no peace march. No, if anything, it was an antagonistic display of what we, the marchers, considered our 'moral superiority,' and in the minds of our detractors a reflexive and at best arrogant, if not treasonous, display of disloyalty.

I marched that hot October morning until I reached the first clouds of tear gas a few blocks from the bridge. Now tired, thirsty, and dripping in sweat, I decided to turn back and walk the 30 or so blocks to the seminary in the hope I would not be recognized as a protestor, and therefore, not be further harassed. But because nothing about my dress or my person distinguished me from anyone else, be it a protestor or a red-blooded " love it or leave it" American, I blended into the crowd with my eyes stinging from the gas and my throat now as dry as Texas sand.

Approaching 29th Street, I spied 'an oasis' in the midst of the desert that was my soul and also at the street intersection before me. Someone was serving ice-cold lemonade to all who passed by. A simple hand-painted sign proclaimed the kingdom of God in these two words: "FREE LEMONADE!"

As I drew closer I could see, even through my bloodshot eyes, our revered professor, Dr. Currie stood there, smiling behind a little makeshift lemonade stand. He handed out free cups of cold liquid refreshment to anyone and to everyone who requested a cup.

People, who hours before had perceived each other as enemies, now gathered around a tiny table bearing large barrels of lemonade. And they joked and laughed and even served each other in a spirit of newfound joy. Every departure was marked by handshakes, smiles, and backslaps and each new arrival was served lemonade without either hesitation or qualifying questions.

And in that moment, I witnessed perhaps the most vivid illustration of peacemaking it has ever been my privilege to discover. For in refusing to hate and also in refusing to take sides, this man demonstrated to the world, in a way I will never forget, that all real and lasting peace can only come from the Kingdom Jesus proclaimed.

CHAPTER 6

The Discovery

I don't believe I needed to write this book in order to discover the answer to my friend's question as to the point of this life we've been given. I could have turned to him and said, "The point is to love, and more specifically, the point is to grow so mature spiritually that our very beings become building blocks, if you will, for the kingdom Jesus proclaimed."

In the simplest way I know to say it: We are to become the Kingdom of God right here and right now. We have been made for love's highest purposes and for love's greatest ends, and if we fail to discern this purpose for our lives, we will likely wander aimlessly about in a wasteland of bewilderment, which is that narrow stretch separating deep satisfaction from abject despair.

Yes, I could have said all of this to my friend, but I chose not to for at least three reasons:

1. To say all of this to him would have been to preach, which is something I had neither the right to do nor the appropriate circumstances for.

2. I felt his deep pain, and in such moments listening is

always the best form of proclamation,

and finally,

3. I knew this friend as a man of such deep faith that I trusted him and the Holy Spirit to collaborate in the discovery of this truth for himself. His unexpected presence at my beloved brother's funeral was a step on the path toward his discovery of an answer to the question he brought with him to John's graveside.

My four-year old grandson, Henry, is fond of offering our family's table grace each time we sit down to dinner together. He often recites the following prayer: "Thank you for the lovely dinner, and thank you for our snacks, our desserts, and for love. Amen."

I can think of no better way to conclude this book than to join Henry in thanking God for love. And as Henry would say, "Amen!"

About the Author

Bob Lively is a native Texan, who was born, raised and educated in the Dallas public schools. He is a graduate of Austin College and also of Austin Presbyterian Theological Seminary. The Presbyterian Church ordained him in 1973, and for the past four decades he has served the church as a pastor, community activist, teacher, certified pastoral counselor, campus minister, and recovery center chaplain.

He is the author of 9 books of non-fiction and is an award-winning short story writer. For 23 years he wrote a regular column in the *Austin American-Statesman*.

The Thin Place is his first novel.

Today he is retired and lives with his wife, Mary Lynn, a former university associate dean, on an acre in the Hill Country west of Austin. He has been named a distinguished alumnus of both Austin College and Austin Seminary.

Made in the USA
Lexington, KY
10 September 2017